Social Rules and
Social Behaviour

Social Rules and Social Behaviour

Edited by Peter Collett

ROWMAN AND LITTLEFIELD
Totowa, New Jersey

First published in the United States 1977
by ROWMAN AND LITTLEFIELD, Totowa, N. J.

© Basil Blackwell 1977

Library of Congress Cataloging in Publication Data
Main entry under title:

Social rules and social behaviour.

    Bibliography: p.
      1. Social norms—Addresses, essays, lectures.
2. Social interaction—Addresses, essays, lectures.
3. Structural linguistics—Addresses, essays, lectures.
4. Children—Language—Addresses, essays, lectures.
5. Semantics (Philosophy)—Addresses, essays, lectures.
I. Collett, Peter.
GN493.3.S65   1976   310.2/1   76-29001
ISBN 0-87471-903-8

Printed in Great Britain

Contents

Preface

The papers collected together in this volume were presented in a seminar of the same title that was held in the Department of Experimental Psychology at Oxford. The series was organised because it was felt that it would be worthwhile reappraising the notion of 'rule' and examining the ways in which it was currently being put to use in different disciplines. To this end speakers from a variety of disciplines were invited to address themselves to a topic connected with the subject of social rules. These papers were later mimeographed and they enjoyed a limited circulation before being re-drafted for publication in the present volume. Parts of some of the essays contained in this collection will be found elsewhere. Sections of Robin Fox's paper appear in his *Encounter with Anthropology* (Penguin, 1975) and Jerome Bruner's paper has also appeared in the *Journal of Child Language* (1975). I owe a debt of thanks to Mrs. Ann McKendry for her assistance in typing up the papers.

Peter Collett

The Rules of Conduct
PETER COLLETT

The idea that social behaviour is in some sense 'governed' by rules is of course an old one. It lies at the basis of the popular belief that there are socially 'correct' or 'proper' ways of behaving, and hence occasionally finds expression in our attempts to either censure others or excuse ourselves through an appeal to such standards. Apart from—or possibly because of—its role in everyday accounts of behaviour, the notion of 'rule' has found it way into academic discourse, where it has been variously used to explain people's expectations of others and/or the regularity of their social behaviours on analogy with the moves of a game or some other formally constituted practice. The idea that certain behaviours are explicable in terms of rules may be found in the works of Kant, Spencer, Saussure and others. In this century it has been advanced most notably by Wittgenstein and Chomsky, who together introduced the notion of rule to the study of language and, through this, to investigations of non-linguistic behaviour.

Although the idea of convention, and with it the distinction between the laws of men and those of nature, may be found in Aristotle, it was really not until Hume (1739) that we find the notion of rule invoked to explain the establishment and maintenance of convention. Kant was probably the first to fully recognise the explanatory power of the notion when he spoke of 'constitutive' and 'regulative' rules in the *Critique of Pure Reason* (1781). Spencer (1879) later drew on the notion when he proposed that it was through adherence to the rules of conduct that custom is upheld. Spencer believed that these rules are part of the organic nature of society; they constitute 'the government of ceremonial observance', a government which preceded all other forms of government and therefore all other systems of rules. The linguist Saussure (1916) was, as far as we know, the first to compare languages and games, although it should be noted that Humboldt (1836), the father of the linguistic relativity hypothesis, had before that offered an elaborate formulation of language as a system of rules or *System von Regeln*. In Saussure's attempt to throw light on the generative character of language and the inter-dependence of linguistic signs, he was drawn to compare language with a game of chess. He argued that, like a game of chess, language consists of a finite set of rules which is capable of generating an infinite set of combinations, and that like the position of a chess piece, each linguistic sign derives its value or meaning from its opposition to all other signs. Thus, in two independent sweeps of the board, Humboldt and Saussure together managed to anticipate much of what was later to be found in Wittgenstein's (1953) treatment of 'language games' and Chomsky's (1965) theory of generative grammar. At the same time Saussure also laid the foundations for what was later to become the corner-stone of structuralism, namely the idea that the properties of a part—whether it be a phoneme in structural linguistics or a character in the study of myth—are defined by its position in a structure.

It is widely agreed that Wittgenstein is responsible for the contemporary interest in rules. The idea of the rule may be found in his conception of language games and his attempts to analyse what it is that underlies our judgements of correct procedure. But, more importantly, it was given a central position in his private language argument. For Wittgenstein the rule was primarily social in nature. It inheres in convention which is corporate, and it is therefore only through the operation of rules that language is capable of dealing in meanings which can be conveyed by, and are comprehensible to, the members of a linguistic community. It is probably not unfair to suggest that Wittgenstein's contribution to our current preoccupation with the rule-concept derives more from its place in an original and influential philosophy than it does from his having undertaken any explicit formulation or detailed analysis of the notion. Nevertheless, it is true to say that Wittgenstein's influence, like that of Chomsky after him, has been far reaching. Chomsky's attraction to the idea of rules arose out of his attempt to secure a conceptual device that would describe the generative work that characterises natural language. For Chomsky, this capacity for language production was innate. The rules served to

describe the transformations that occurred at the syntactic level in the
deep structure, and his discovery procedure consisted in constructing a
model of the rules that would most elegantly and economically generate
those sentences which the native speaker deemed to be grammatically
admissible. So one finds in Chomsky these interesting symmetries,
already discussed by Humboldt and Saussure and hinted at by Wittgenstein, between production and comprehension within the speaker-
hearer and among members of the same linguistic community; the
same rules of syntax serve both to produce and interpret sentences.
Another interesting point is that the prime criterion for Chomsky was
that of grammaticality; there is in his early work this assumption that
the linguistic base is a syntactic one, a supposition that has since been
seriously challenged by generative semanticists like Fillmore (1968) and
sociolinguists like Hymes (1971).

It is not easy to determine precisely the paths of influence along which
the rule-concept has been conveyed to us today. And in this sense its
historical development has been somewhat like the diffuse course of
some subterranean waterway, erupting in the work of one author and
then, years later, reappearing in a seemingly unrelated fashion in the
works of others. If our speculative water-divining is correct, it would
seem that there have been two main streams of influence. The one
stream may be traced from Humboldt and Saussure to the Prague
School of Linguistics and thence both to Lévi-Strauss and contemporary structural anthropology and to Chomsky and transformational
linguistics, while the other may be seen as originating in Wittgenstein,
from whom it flowed into linguistic philosophy. It looks as though it
was the joint influence of structural anthropology and transformational
linguistics which introduced the rule-concept to cognitive anthropology, and that it was the same two branches which, together with
the tributary influence of Schutz and George Herbert Mead, brought
the idea to modern interpretative sociology. Today there is something
of a delta formation in the social sciences, with a proliferation of
schools that appear to be more the product of some neologistic frenzy
than any diversity of subject-matter. Ethnoscientists, ethnosemanti-
cists, formal and componential analysts, ethnomethodologists, symbolic interactionists and phenomenological sociologists have all been
swimming around happily with the idea of rules for some time now.
Social psychologists, always eager but wary, have however only
begun to paddle in the shallow water.

Despite the enthusiasm with which the notion of rules has been received and the breadth of its present application, the idea has been employed quite uncritically and, in many cases, indiscriminately. Seldom have attempts been made to specify what exactly is meant by the term. It therefore seems advisable that we pause for a moment to consider the various meanings of the term 'rule', and that we examine what it is we commit ourselves to when we use the term in one of its various senses.

It has been pointed out that rules have no truth value, and that they are conditional and prescriptive. There are various types of rules, and these may be distinguished from scientific 'laws', in that laws have truth value and are not prescriptive. More importantly, laws cannot be violated, whereas it is a fundamental requirement of a rule that it can be broken. This is the condition of *breach*. Another more contentious requirement is that rules be capable of change. This is the condition of *alteration*. It is captured in Waismann's point that one of the essential characteristics of rules is their arbitrariness; a rule 'is arbitrary, not because it has actually been chosen, but because there is always the possibility of cancelling it, or replacing it by another' (1965 : 140). Much the same idea is found in Oakeshott's contention that the moral life involves 'conduct to which there is an alternative' (quoted in Winch, 1971 : 65), and in Lewis' (1969) suggestion that convention can only arise where there is more than one 'coordinate equilibrium', that is, more than one way in which people could collectively coordinate their activities toward the achievement of some end. We may be tempted at this point to insist that the arbitrary character of a rule be acknowledged by members of the community which upholds the rule; that alternative solutions, rather than being extrinsically defined, be seen as alternatives by people in that community. However, there is sufficient evidence to show that people often regard the rules of conduct in their society as anything but arbitrary; many rules are regarded as immutable, if not God-given. In advocating the condition of alteration, we would therefore require a weaker criterion, one which allowed for the *possibility* of alternative solutions being specified by members of the society, and one in which responsibility is placed on the investigator to demonstrate that such alternatives are logically possible.

This brings us to the question of whether or not all rules satisfy the condition of alteration, that is whether or not the alternatives to established practice are logically feasible. In this connection, Winch (1972) has argued that there are some rules which are essential to human society and which therefore could not be changed. He offers the example of the rule against lying, and suggests that although people frequently abstain from telling the truth, nevertheless a society which did not uphold truthfulness, or whose members continually lied, would not be viable. There is of course an obvious sense in which the general rule against lying is quite unlike the rule which requires that one drive on the left side of the road, or the way in which, say, the incest taboo is quite unlike the rule which prescribes that men wear black tie on certain formal occasions. It is probably fair to say that rules against lying and incest prescribe behaviours which, as Fox (this volume) suggests, would not have occurred or not have occurred that frequently, even in the absence of the rule. Necessary rules such as these are statements after the fact. They derive their prescriptive power by being commentaries on necessary states of affairs, whereas contingent rules such as those which govern the way one drives or the apparel one wears are either deliberately instituted or else arise through some custom which could have been otherwise. But even then the picture is too simply drawn. Winch's argument is of course a convincing one, but only by virtue of its presupposing a single unitary rule against lying rather than a variety of rules for and against lying. While it is undoubtedly the case that all societies espouse truthfulness in its broadest sense, it is certainly not the case that they require it in all circumstances. In our own society there are situations in which lying is condoned, if not prescribed. When, for example, the boss's wife asks how you like her new hair-style, your correct response is to offer favourable comment, not to display your capacity for honesty.

Apart from being open to infringement, and in some cases change, rules may have various other properties. Kant, we have noted, distinguished between constitutive and regulative rules. The distinction is important and, not surprisingly, may therefore be found in the writings of several contemporary authors, despite the fact that they occasionally differ from both Kant and each other in their use of the terms (see Black, 1962; Schwayder, 1965; Searle, 1970). For our purposes we will assume that a constitutive rule defines or constitutes a practice, while a regulative rule guides or regulates behaviour. So, for example, a constitutive rule in rugby might be 'A try is scored when the ball in play is grounded in the opponents' in-goal area', and a regulative rule in polite society might be 'Gentlemen should rise to their feet when a lady enters the room'. We notice that a constitutive rule is essentially definitional, that it indicates what counts as what and at the same time gives meaning to actions which are performed according to that rule. In the case of the rugby example the constitutive rule specifies what may count as a try. It also defines any action which satisfies the rule as a try rather than mere placement of a ball on the grass. But the constitutive rule governing tries does not stand alone. Only by being embedded in a system of rules which constitutes the game of rugby, does it assign meaning to a try within the context of the game as a whole. Regulative rules, on the other hand, do not constitute social practices. Instead, they inform individuals as to what should be done. As Searle puts it, they take the formulation *If P, then Q*, while constitutive rules take the formulation *X counts as Y*.

There has been some debate as to the relation between constitutive and regulative rules. Some theorists (e.g. Black, 1962) have insisted that all rules can be reduced to regulative rules, while others (e.g. Gumb, 1972) have proposed that constitution and regulation are really properties of all rules. Both of these arguments reveal part of the picture, for one can see how each type of rule can be forced to fit the formulation of the other, and at the same time how regulative rules depend upon the definitional properties of purely constitutive rules. That is, the rule which requires that gentlemen stand up when a lady enters the room could only regulate behaviour if gentlemen had mastered a rule or a system of rules which enabled them to recognise what counts as a lady. We may conclude then that the two types of rule are heuristically distinguishable, and that while constitutive rules do not regulate activities, nevertheless regulative rules do require the assistance of constitutive rules. At this stage it should be pointed out that in what follows we will be dealing largely with regulative rules that either prescribe or proscribe various forms of social conduct.

If we take a simple formulation of a regulative rule, *If P, then Q*, then we can speak of the conditions (*P*) that render a class of behaviours (*Q*) obligatory, permissible or prohibited for a particular category of persons. It is evident that the formulation offered above is also a formulation of a physical law. So we need to add that the term 'then' is to be understood as prescribing, permitting or proscribing certain actions rather than as describing them. In the case of prescriptive and proscriptive rules (which are intertranslatable and which henceforth will both be called 'prescriptive') the word 'then' implies 'should' or 'ought' and therefore 'can'. However, in the case of permissive rules, such as certain legal rules which empower people to act in a particular fashion, the term 'then' implies 'may'.[1] The prescriptive component of rules—what Wittgenstein referred to as the 'compulsion' of a rule, and what Black and Ganz have in turn called the 'push' or 'prescriptive force' of a rule—derives from the critical role of the community which upholds the rule and its power to administer sanction and reward or, where the rule has been internalised, the critical role of the self as a member of that community. In formulations such as that above, the expression P serves, as a kind of blanket term, to subsume all the salient preconditions such as time, place, persons and so forth, while the expression Q serves to describe the salient aspects of the behaviour that is called for, disallowed, or permitted by the set P. The term 'salient' is essential here because the formulation of a rule describes, or at least should describe, only the minimal set of preconditions, and the minimal behaviour that will satisfy that rule. So, for example, the rules for check-mate refer neither to the colour of the dark squares on the chess board, nor to the hand that is used to effect the move, although it is invariably the case that chess boards have black squares and chess players use their right hand to move the pieces.

We have here an illustration of the point made by Wittgenstein and later reiterated by Winch, namely that the words 'same' and 'rule' are inextricably linked. They are linked because constitutive rules define what counts as the same and what counts as different, and because regulative rules rely on constitutive rules to define their Ps and Qs. So, in the case of forms of address, a regulative rule might prescribe that older men be addressed as 'Sir', in which case constitutive rules would define what counts as an older male and what counts as an acceptable utterance of the address. We have suggested that regulative rules entail constitutive rules. But then again, constitutive rules do not stand in isolation. Instead, they too point to other constitutive rules which in turn serve to define their constituent parts. This suggests that in the process of learning a language, or for that matter any rule-governed behaviour, the acquisition of certain rules will be predicated upon prior acquisition of other rules which contain the constitutive definitions necessary for their mastery. In other words, one could only appreciate what it means to score a try if one had already grasped the

1. The idea that 'ought' implies 'can' is Kantian. Although social rules invariably prescribe conduct which is humanly possible, there are certain rules of liability in law which violate the relationship between 'ought' and 'can'. Hart points out that the Law does not always take account of the ability of individuals to fulfil its requirements.

idea of a game and before that had acquired an understanding of the constituents of the game such as player, opponent, etc.

It has been noted that rules are 'prescriptive'. This does not imply that they have some mysterious autonomy of their own which enables them to pass judgement on the deeds of men. Rather, what is meant is that prescriptive rules specify 'correct' or 'appropriate' procedures, and that the members of a community which upholds a rule will, as it were, reserve for themselves the right to evaluate the performance of those individuals whom they take to fall within its jurisdiction. Here the community which evaluates need not be the same as that class of persons to whom the rule refers. In fact there are four possible types of relationship between such a community and such a class of persons, these being relationships of 'correspondence', 'class inclusion', 'community inclusion' and 'separation'. These are depicted below, with squares standing for the community, and circles for the class of persons over whom the community assumes the rule legitimately to hold sway. In passing, it might be worth noting that there are several interesting structural properties of these relationships: in cases of correspondence

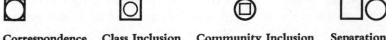

Correspondence   Class Inclusion   Community Inclusion   Separation

and class inclusion the individual to whom the rule refers is likely to feel that the community's expectations are warranted or justified, while in instances of community inclusion and separation various social and political tensions are likely to arise between those who espouse the rule and those who reject its legitimacy.

Rules are upheld, though not necessarily observed, by a community. They derive their existence in the minds of people through the shared belief that other individuals value the rule. This is not to say that all rules are social rules. Contrary to Wittgenstein's contention, there may be 'private rules', although—and this is Schwayder's point—such private rules may depend on the prior existence of social or corporate rules. There are various possible relationships between an individual and a social rule, such that he may either know the rule or not know the rule, and his behaviour may either accord with the rule or contravene the rule. This two-fold distinction may be represented as follows:

	Person does not know the rule	Person knows the rule
Person's behaviour does not accord with the rule	A	C
Person's behaviour does accord with the rule	B	D

Before considering the four types of relationship presented in this diagram, we shall first discuss what it means to speak of someone as knowing a rule. We shall then direct our attention to each of the four types of relationship in turn.

Several commentators on rules have referred to the fact that there are various kinds of rules. Not only are there legal rules, moral and religious rules, linguistic rules, social norms, rules of etiquette, rules of games and rules of institutions, but there are also recipes, instructions, formulae, canons, principles and maxims (see Rommetveit, 1955; Gibbs, 1955; Black, 1962; von Wright, 1963; Goffman, 1971). Furthermore, rules may originate in a variety of ways. They may arise through legal enactment, informal agreement, convention or the suggestion of an influential individual. Typically writers who have tried to bring some order to the various notions that fall under the rubric 'rule' have proposed that they be distinguished, at least initially, in terms of whether or not they have been promulgated by a properly installed authority, and whether or not their violation permits the invocation of some sanction. But in concerning ourselves with different types of rules, we would probably be better advised to consider not so much the formal distinctions of authority and permissible sanction, but rather the definitions of rules inasmuch as these are grounded in different empirical procedures for recognising a rule as a particular type of rule. When we speak of an individual as knowing a rule, we can mean several things, and depending on which criteria we employ when we attribute knowledge of a rule to an individual, we can end up with different kinds of rules. There are at least four senses in which an individual can be said to know a rule.

The first sense of knowing a rule involves being able to articulate some recognisable formulation of the rule. For example, when someone is being tested for his driving licence he must be able to specify what kinds of behaviour are required, permissible or prohibited under certain conditions. This, then, is the criterion of *articulation*.

The second sense of knowing a rule involves being able to recognise infringements of the rule. Chomsky, for instance, would attribute knowledge of a grammatical rule to someone provided he could distinguish syntactically correct from incorrect utterances involving that rule. Chomsky would require demonstration of ability to recognise breaches of the rule rather than articulation of the rule; he would only be interested, as he puts it, in 'what the speaker actually knows, not what he reports about his knowledge' (1965 : 8). Notice here that an inability to satisfy either the condition of articulation or that of *recognition* would lead one to suppose that the person did not know the rule, and that the first requirement is the more demanding of the two.

The third sense in which someone might be said to know a rule involves his applying a *sanction* whenever the rule is broken. That is, it might be suggested that the difference between behaviours which are governed by a rule and those which are not so governed consists in the fact that departures from the former, but not the latter type, are met by applications of sanction to the offending party. In so far as applications of sanction by an individual depends upon his having already recognised a breach of the rule, this third sense is related to that discussed immediately above. The criterion of sanction has been employed by legal philosophers. It is also common to the discovery procedures of ethnomethodologists like Garfinkel (1963, 1967) and the validation procedures of cognitive anthropologists such as Goodenough (1967). Garfinkel and his students have used a wide variety of rule-breaking techniques ranging from mild disruptions of games of noughts and crosses to more dramatic disturbances of family life in which a student adopts the role of guest in his own home. In the case of noughts and crosses, for example, the rule-breaker might deliberately place his nought or cross on the line, rather than between the lines, and any consequent disapproval or demand for retraction by his opponent would be taken to indicate the operation of a rule against the placement of noughts and crosses on the lines. Similarly, if a student offered to pay his mother for her hospitality after dinner and she in turn expressed some bewilderment, then her response would be regarded as evidence in support of the inference that there was a rule against such behaviour. The relationship of the cognitive anthropologists to the notion of sanction has been somewhat different from this. Several cognitive anthropologists have suggested that one way in which an ethnographer might validate his model of the rules of a community might be to act in accordance with them. It is assumed that to the extent that he has correctly identified the cultural grammar of that community (and of course managed to act in accordance with it), he will avoid criticism from members of that community for having violated their social rules (Goodenough, 1967; Tyler, 1969).

The fourth and final sense of knowing a rule would occur where an inference about the operation of a rule was made purely on the basis of some observed *behavioural regularity*. Having, for example, observed that people in England drive on the left side of the road, one might, without bothering to discuss the matter with English drivers, decide that there was a rule to that effect.

These then, are the four bases for attributing knowledge of a rule to someone. The first thing we notice is that the criteria of articulation and recognition involved—admittedly in quite different ways—a specification of the rule by the agent, whereas the criteria of sanction and behavioural regularity involve an inference about the rule by the trained observer or 'recognised expert'. The difference between these loci of rule-specification parallels Pike's (1967) distinction between *emic* and *etic* descriptions. In the first two instances attribution of knowledge of the rule is based on an appeal to the intuitions of the actor, while in the third and fourth cases it is founded on the critical observations and inferences of someone who stands outside the stage. In the last two cases such trained observers may believe that the testimony of the actor is irrelevant, or they may feel, along with Durkheim (1897), that it is uninformative or potentially misguided.

Thus far we have discussed what it means to speak of someone as knowing a rule, and already we can see that there may be disagreements as to the circumstances under which a person may properly be said to know a rule. Now we may be tempted to define knowledge of a rule in terms of someone behaving in some regular fashion, but were we to do so we would soon find ourselves in the ridiculous predicament of not being able to distinguish between behaviours which are governed by rules and those which are not so governed, and where we would have to reject the possibility of there being rules which were either infrequently followed or not followed at all. Clearly, not all regular behaviours are governed by rules. For example, all the members of a group may regularly drink tea at breakfast or go weekly to the cinema, and yet, as Hart (1961) points out, there are no rules that prescribe periodic consumption of tea or regular attendance at the cinema.

There are even more problems associated with the criterion of sanction. The most serious of these consists in the fact that not all rules are linked to sanctions. Certainly neither constitutive rules nor permissive regulative rules are. But even when we consider prescriptive regulative rules (i.e. those which either prescribe or prohibit behaviour), we find that the procedures for establishing what is and what is not sanction are often unclear. One can see how actions which appear at first sight to be sanctions might in fact not be, and how punishment or criticism which is not related to infringement of a rule might therefore readily be misconstrued as sanction. Black (1968) has argued that linguistic rules have an imperative force because they are supported by sanction. To illustrate his point he has suggested that violators of such rules are penalised in that they run the risk of being misunderstood. Now although we might be prepared to concede that certain prescriptive regulative rules are backed by sanction, I think we should be extremely hesitant about Black's characterisation, for it is at once far too loose and contrary to what we understand by the term sanction. One might wish to suggest that all prescriptive regulative rules can ultimately be linked to sanction, even if the penalty that is reserved for their infraction is no more than polite correction, but this is a far cry from assuming that any untoward consequence which arises from infringement of a rule may be regarded as a sanction. When we speak of sanction we should take care to limit our discussion to those forms of social retribution which are administered by some party or parties (possibly including the violator himself) who act, or could legitimately act, solely with the breach in mind. This requirement, that sanction be identified solely in terms of those actions which are designed to be retributive in relation to the infringement of a rule, is however not without its problems, for there is a sense in which, at least from the actor's point of view, *any* deleterious event which follows on the heels of an immoral act may be regarded as a sanction meted out by some metaphysical agency. The poor beleaguered Israelites of the Old Testament saw their misfortunes as the visitations of a wrathful God, and even today there are people of a religious or superstitious frame of mind who will readily construe their personal mishaps as the consequences of their earlier transgressions.

Another problem which arises in connection with the proposal that rules be inferred from the administration of sanction is that sanctions are not automatically applied when rules which are backed by sanction are broken. Therefore any reliance upon applications of sanction by persons who witness supposed infringements of a rule will fail to disclose those rules whose threat of sanction is not carried out. Even where sanction or criticism is forthcoming, it is extremely difficult to say what rule, if any rule at all, has been broken. Supposing, for example, that my family and I regularly drink tea at breakfast, and that one morning I decide to break with habit and have coffee instead. Would repeated exhortations or teasing on the part of my family constitute sanction? Could I in fact be said to have broken a rule? I think not. Finally, there are procedural difficulties related to the identification of rules through the method of active breach. How, for example, is the rule-breaker to ensure that his deliberate breach is not accompanied by some other bizarre behaviour to which people are reacting, and how is the observer of naturally occurring breaches to discount the explanation that people who violate the rules elicit criticism, not for having broken the rules, but because they are regarded as unsavoury or undesirable for some other reason?

Breaches of the rule are not always followed by applications of sanction. If anything, there are separate systems of rules governing the invocation of sanction in the event of a rule being broken. Most of the rules governing applications of sanction appear to be permissive, although there are of course instances where a person who fails to apply sanctions may in turn be sanctioned or chastised by the transgressor or some third party. A rather esoteric instance of a mandatory rule governing application of sanction may be found in the game of checkers. Braybrooke tells us that 'a player who can take an opposing piece and fails to do so lays himself open to the penalty of the "huff". This means that his opponent can remove from the board the man or king which should have made the capture' (1968 : 334). There is no necessary relationship between instances where a rule is broken and instances where a sanction is applied. In fact people repeatedly demonstrate a rather high level of tolerance for infractions of the rules which would appear, at least to the outsider, to be strangely inconsistent with what would be expected, given just an understanding of the rules and the sanctions permissible in cases of their contravention. There seems to be a system of socially sustained, almost necessary, thresholds beyond which breaches are 'commonly' recognised and responded to with criticisms or requests for retraction. We repeatedly make grammatical mistakes in our speech and yet we are seldom reproached by other people. For that matter, we seldom notice, let alone correct, the mistakes of others. Instead we allow these things to pass, for were we less permissive than we are, conversation would be a far more stilted affair than it is.

Given that there are serious problems associated with the criteria of behavioural regularity and sanction, both of these should be abandoned in favour of either the criterion of articulation or that of recognition. Now both Quine (1972) and caution would advise that we adopt the former criterion, but a critical inspection of the contradictions which attend its use would recommend the criterion of recognition to us, for it is sufficiently clear that there are instances in which an individual who manifestly knows the rule will not describe it or not be able to describe it. Black offers us the example of the chess player who knows that no two pieces may occupy the same square simultaneously, but who, even when pressed, would be unlikely to list this rule among the rules of chess. Equally, there are instances in which individuals respond adversely to the behaviours of others without being able to specify precisely the behaviours of which they disapproved nor the behaviours which they would have preferred. After all, rules are not merely the property of the articulate.

With that much said, let us for the moment accept that we are prepared to attribute knowledge of a rule to someone provided he can formulate something like the rule or, following Winch, that he can recognise instances of its breach. It will not be necessary to require that the individual commonly externalises his recognitions of breach or that he behaves in accordance with the rule, but only that under certain controlled eliciting conditions he reliably demonstrates an ability to distinguish behaviours which contravene the rule from those which are in accordance with the rule. Those individuals who cannot satisfy such requirements will be deemed to be ignorant of the rule.

Let us now return to our four-fold table and consider those instances where an individual can be said to either know or not know a rule and where his behaviour can be seen to either conform to that rule or contravene that rule.

A. *Where the Person is Ignorant of the Rule and*
   where his Behaviour Contravenes the Rule

If an individual cannot be said to have knowledge of a rule and if at the same time his behaviour fails to conform to a rule, then it makes little sense to speak of his behaviour as being rule-governed. Instances in which the rule is broken by those who are ignorant of it exhibit certain interesting properties, some of which we shall discuss below.

B. *Where the Person is Ignorant of the Rule and*
   where his Behaviour Accords with the Rule

The mere fact that behaviour is congruent with a rule does not justify its being explained in terms of the rule. Of course, we may some day discover one of those proverbial monkeys that had managed, after years at the typewriter, to reproduce a line from one of Shakespeare's sonnets. But just as we would not be prepared to credit it with a knowledge of Elizabethan English, so too we would not allow that those social behaviours which conform to the requirements of a rule are necessarily to be explained by reference to it. There are undoubtedly many instances where people behave in such a way as to make their actions comprehensible in terms of a rule; yet if they are unaware of the rule then clearly another type of explanation is called for. It is probably the case that a great deal of public, especially ceremonial or ritual, behaviour is of this character, so that initiates are prompted through sequences of behaviour which appear, on the face of it, to be 'rule-guided' where they are actually only 'rule-fitting' (Quine, 1972).

Some of us may recall those occasions at polite dinner parties where one found oneself confronted by an indistinguishable array of cutlery, and where one was only able to select the correct knife and fork, and thereby avert embarrassment, through timely imitation of the host or some other guest. In so doing, one might have performed adequately, giving the impression of knowing the rule where one was in fact quite ignorant of it. Now some might wish to contend that such imitative behaviour is itself rule-governed; in other words that there is a rule prescribing mimicry of the host in circumstances of ignorance. But this is not the case. Rather, there is a social requirement that one *somehow* determine what is correct behaviour without revealing one's ignorance to others, and that one then act upon this information. Were a book on etiquette readily available, and had one developed sufficient slight of hand, one could just as easily look up the appropriate behaviour for that occasion.

Two important points follow from the dinner party illustration.

Firstly, it is evident that imitation in instances such as the dinner party arises out of an assumption on the part of the guest as to the existence of a rule, although it should be noted that imitation does not itself necessarily indicate that the person entertains such an assumption. If, for example, I know that you are an expert rambler, I may follow you up the mountain side, not because I take there to be a rule governing rambling, but because I assume you know the easiest path. The second point concerns the relationship between the imitator and the rule. Clearly, someone who succeeds in imitating a piece of rule-governed behaviour need never actually acquire an understanding of the rule that governs that behaviour. True enough, he may, by his actions, show that he appreciates the requisite behaviour, or what would be the Q in the formulation of the rule, but he may still not be able to discern the precise nature of the preconditions and therefore the relationship between P and Q. Presumably what happens is that the imitator forms an inductive hypothesis about the rule and then tests this against subsequent instances until he arrives at an hypothesis that resists disconfirmation. For example, supposing our rather clueless guest was served trout for first course and, finding himself ignorant of the correct procedure, he were to imitate the host and use the fish knife and fork. He might assume thereafter that such cutlery is reserved specifically for first courses, in which case he would prove to be sadly mistaken were he to act on that assumption when served melon for first course on a later occasion. Obviously there are several different inferences that our guest could have drawn about the nature of the rule, but were he to have assumed that the fish knife and fork were used for fish dishes then he would in time have been able to derive some consolation from the fact that his rule-inference did not appear to be incorrect. However, were he less eager to conceal his ignorance and were he to enquire about the rule then he would have the added satisfaction of knowing that his initial conjecture had in fact been correct. It would seem that in the absence of instruction by rule we may be somewhat like Quine's (1960) linguist who finds himself among a hitherto untouched people whose language has never been translated. The linguist observes that when a rabbit scurries by, the natives says 'Gavagai', and he jots down 'Rabbit' in his notebook. Now just as the linguist's translation would remain a tentative one until it was shown to be incorrect, so too rules which are acquired through inference rather than enquiry can only wait on disconfirmation. This does not mean that whenever we infer a rule we are necessarily aware of the inductive procedure we have employed or the tentative nature of the inference we have drawn. In fact, as far as the person is concerned, an inference which has not been disconfirmed is probably as good as one that has been confirmed.

C. *Where the Person Knows the Rule and where his Behaviour Contravenes the Rule*

A rule can only be violated where the antecedent conditions hold. If we examine those instances where an agent can reliably be shown to know a rule, but fails to display the behaviour required by the rule, we find that various explanations can be offered. The most obvious of these is the case of the agent who *chooses* to behave in a manner other than that prescribed by the rule. He might, for example, jump the bus queue because he had promised to be elsewhere, or because he wished to flaunt his disregard for convention. I would like to suggest that we have here two conceptually distinct types of reason for deliberate breach of a social rule, such that it may arise as much out of a desire to act for another rule as out of a desire to act for another reason which is not related to a rule. The predicament of the man who finds himself simultaneously under the jurisdiction of two competing social rules is of course an interesting one. It is a problem that was acknowledged by Kierkegaard, and which has since been elaborated by Sartre and Simone de Beauvoir. Sartre offers us the example of the young Frenchman during the German occupation who is faced with the dilemma of choosing between joining the resistance and looking after his ageing mother.[2] Deliberate breach is not the only reason for discrepancy between the prescriptions of a rule and the behaviour of someone who knows the rule. In fact, if we return to our original formulation of a rule then we notice that contraventions may also arise through misconstrual of the antecedent conditions and/or through an inability on the part of the agent to engage in the requisite behaviour.

Not all rules offer an unambiguous specification of the preconditions that call for a piece of behaviour; it is often difficult to know whether the conditions for a rule obtain. This haziness or ambiguity of condi-

2. In social psychology and sociology this problem has appeared in the study of 'role strain' and the resolution of 'role-conflict' (see Secord & Backman, 1974). The concept of rule is of course closely linked to that of role, such that a role may be thought of as a bundle of rules, and an assemblage of rules as constituting a role.

tionals was noted by Wittgenstein, who observed that rules sometimes leave room for doubt. 'It is only in normal cases that the use of a word is clearly prescribed; we know, are in no doubt, what to say in this or that case. The more abnormal the case, the more doubtful it becomes what to say' (1953 : 56). Hart has also spoken of the 'penumbra of uncertainty' that surrounds a rule. The other type of reason for unintended disparity between the behaviour prescribed by a rule and the actual behaviour displayed by the agent is that of inability. It is evident that one may know the rule, observe that certain conditions which call for a particular piece of behaviour hold, and yet be unable to produce the behaviour in question. A referee may be a clumsy player, a baritone may lose his voice, and the archbishop may trip at the altar. Yet we would not be inclined to say that these people were ignorant of the rules associated with their respective pursuits, nor that their violations of the rules were in any meaningful sense of the word deliberate. This underlines the fact that our everyday assessments of other people are irrevocably bound up with attributions of intentions and abilities to them. These judgements are of course also bound up with inferences concerning their knowledge of the rules and with inferences concerning their perceptions of the conditions that call forth the actions required by the rules.[3] That is, those sanctions that are reserved for infringement of a social rule will usually be cancelled in those cases where we infer that the transgressor does not know the rule, did not correctly perceive the preconditions of the rule, is without the necessary ability to follow the rule or did not seriously intend to act in a manner contrary to the requirements of the rule. This is not to suggest that sanction will *automatically* be suspended or withheld where such inferences are drawn; only that those who wish, for whatever reason, to administer sanction under such circumstances may need to legitimise their actions by arguing that knowledge, misperception, ability or intention were not absent or that these considerations are irrelevant to the case at hand. Correspondingly, in order to avoid having to punish another, the reluctant administrator of a mandatory

3. The notion of intention is also central to the administration of the law, but interestingly the issue of knowledge of the law is not. There is a branch of jurisprudence, best represented by the work of Hart, which identifies laws with rules. Systems of law, like common rules of conduct, prescribe or proscribe certain practices, and certain laws, like some rules, empower particular individuals to make various decisions which may of course include creating new laws or altering old ones.

sanction will need to either feign an incorrect inference or argue that none of these four requirements were satisfied—as in the case of parents who excuse themselves for not disciplining their children. Similarly, in order to avoid being sanctioned, the miscreant will need to present himself as someone who did not know the rule or possess the requisite abilities. If this does not work he can either claim that he failed to perceive the relevant eliciting conditions or that he did not intend to offend others (cf Lyman and Scott, 1970).

The discrepancy between the prescriptions embodied in a rule and the behaviours of an individual or the members of a community has been notoriously overlooked by students of social behaviour. Indeed, there are ethnographers, in particular structuralists like Lévi-Strauss and Needham and cognitive anthropologists like Frake, Goodenough and Conklin, who hold that it is not the prime task of anthropology to study behaviour, or for that matter any discrepancy between rules and behaviours, but instead to examine cultural categories. In many instances it is either explicitly or tacitly assumed that a description of a rule or a system of rules will be sufficient to indicate likely behaviour. But even the most casual observation should remind us that specification or disclosure of such rules will not necessarily offer any indication of the extent to which they are followed. Evans-Pritchard tells us that among the Nuer there was an inverse relation between commitment to patriliny in principle and commitment to it in deed, and it is equally evident from other quarters that the kinship systems described by native informants are not always those that are practised on the ground. Radcliffe-Brown was sadly mistaken when he insisted that the conscious model was an accurate reflection of group structure.

Just as the attitudes that subjects express to social psychologists may not always be those upon which they act, so too the rules that one might uncover concerning people's conceptions of appropriate behaviour need not be those that are followed in actuality. Both Saussure and Chomsky appreciated this point. Saussure coined the expressions *langue* and *parole*, and Chomsky used the terms *competence* and *performance*, to capture the distinction between ideal systems such as language and actual behaviours such as speech. Interestingly, both of them opted for an exclusive study of the former. Discrepancies between rules and behaviours are borne of people's relationships to the rules and other competing motives. To fob off such discrepancies as being due to some type of limitation or disturbance in the system is merely to ignore the question of what it is that governs behaviour if it is not the rules which people espouse. Malinowski was correct when he noted that the sociologist who relies solely on the native informant's point of view 'obtains at best that lifeless body of laws, regulations, morals and conventionalities which *ought* to be obeyed, but in reality are often only evaded. For in actual life rules are never entirely conformed to, and it remains the most difficult but indispensable part of the ethnographer's work, to ascertain the extent and mechanism of the deviations' (1922 : 428).

We have argued that people do not necessarily behave according to the rules that they know or claim to espouse. It follows, especially in instances where the rule is repeatedly contravened by members of a society, that rules will not, as Bierstedt (1963 : 222) and Schwayder (1965 : 252) suggest, be synonymous with people's expectations. If I know that a rule is repeatedly violated and if therefore I expect you to break that rule, then it makes little sense to speak of a rule as a type of expectation. Similarly, to suggest, as does Schwayder, that a rule only exists in so far as it is followed, is to miss the point. Rules need neither manifest themselves in expectations or behaviours; it is merely sufficient that they serve as a subjective yardstick in the evaluation of behaviour, that they encapsulate cultural notions about correct and incorrect ways of doing things.

Simmel (1950) has an interesting passage in which he suggests that infringement of social rules has particularly serious consequences for both the miscreant and society at large. Such violations, he argues, have consequences 'which are especially grave, which single out the individual from his group'. Social life rests on a set of agreed-upon rules, and although not everybody may be aware of them, nevertheless 'they constitute the minimum of what must be acknowledged by all who want, in any way, to communicate with each other'. Yet, says Simmel, if we examine any one of these rules closely we see that its observance gives us no positive possession at all, for while we derive no distinction from its observance, 'only the *violation* of the norm creates particular and exposed situations, while staying in the norm produces no more than the possibility of remaining within . . . theoretical and practical generality' (: 399). The suggestion here is that because adherence to the rules is crucial to the maintenance of the social process no advantage is conferred upon those individuals who follow the rules. Instead, those who contravene the rules endanger the social process and are therefore liable for sanction. The premise of this argument is, however, false. We have seen that there are rules which are seldom, if ever, observed, and that there are instances where infringements do not in fact produce exposed situations. Furthermore, what Simmel has done is to characterise all social rules as being empowered by the threat of sanction, without admitting of the contrary case, that is, rules which are empowered by the promise of reward.

If we accept this distinction and the possibility that different rules may be differentially empowered, we may then ask, under what conditions do people enhance their reputations by observing the rules but lose nothing by failing to do so, and under what conditions do they derive no special distinction by adhering to the rules but stand in danger of foregoing something by violating them? It would seem that rules which are empowered by the threat of sanction relate to actions which are, in some way, central to the maintenance of the social process, which are relatively easy to perform and/or which are expected of those who fall under the sway of the rule, whereas rules which are empowered by the promise of reward relate to actions which are somehow peripheral to the support of the social process, which are arduous to perform and/or which are not really expected of those who fall within the province of the rule. In other words, the question of whether a rule is empowered by sanction, reward or a combination of sanction and reward will be linked to the *centrality* and *facility* of the required actions as well as the *expectations* that others have in relation to the performance of those actions.

Rules which are empowered by the promise of reward are best exemplified by the variety of religious or secular moral prescriptions which, while being widely endorsed, are seldom observed and, correspondingly, seldom expected of others. In such cases those who follow the rules are invariably rewarded, whereas those who do not are seldom sanctioned. On the other hand, rules which are empowered by sanction are best exemplified by those common rules of etiquette which are widely endorsed, invariably observed and therefore expected of others. Here the individual who conforms to the rule derives no special advantage by his conformity, while he does run the risk of being sanctioned whenever he flouts the rule. Simmel offers us an example which fits this latter case. He refers to the rules that underlie the convention of greeting, and suggests that even 'from their most punctilious observance we must not infer any positive existence of the esteem and devotion they emphasize; but their slightest violation is an unmistakable indication that these feelings do *not* exist. Greeting somebody in the street proves no esteem whatever, but failure to do so conclusively proves the opposite. The forms of courtesy fail as symbols of positive, inner attitudes, but they are most useful in documenting negative ones, since even the slightest omission can radically and definitely alter our relation to a person' (: 400 ff.). That is to say, some actions may derive their signal value from their absence as opposed to their presence; in some instances we may be more informed by what people fail to do rather than what they do. An analogy may be in order at this point. The analogy concerns a study of feral domestic fowl in the wild by McBride *et al.* (1969). They found that when a hen is feeding with her brood, she emits a series of 'clucks' as a location call for maintaining contact with her chicks, and they in turn give 'chirps' for the same reason. Under these circumstances any termination of the hen's clucks or the chicks' chirps will be taken as a sign of trouble. They also observed that other calls, such as 'double clucks' or 'cackling', function equally as an alarm signal. Thus we have in this case two types of signal system, one which we might conveniently term an 'on–off' system, where the *absence* of a steady signal serves as an alarm, the other an 'off–on' system in which the *presence* of a signal serves the same end. This distinction has obvious parallels with that offered earlier. That is, those actions which are related to rules empowered by sanction have the property of an on–off signal system, such that inferences are only drawn from the absence or cessation of an expected act, whereas those actions which are related to rules empowered by reward have the property of an off–on signal system in which inferences are drawn from the presence of an act which was not really anticipated. The repeated clucks and chirps of the hen and chicks serve as a locational device. We may wish to say that just as they express the spatial relationships between the hen and her brood, so too acts like greeting express the social relationships between adherents to that convention.

D. *Where the Person Knows the Rule and*
where his Behaviour Accords with the Rule

Where it can reliably be shown that someone knows a rule, and where this person's behaviour is observed to accord with the rule, there it would seem we have a paradigm instance of rule-governed behaviour. This kind of identity between behaviours prescribed by a rule and behaviours displayed by those who know the rule may derive from at least two types of relationships between a person and a rule: broadly speaking, he may either consult the rule in a reflective fashion, or else he may act on the rule in a relatively unthinking or unreflective fashion. Oakeshott offers this distinction between instances where people consciously select the appropriate behaviour and instances where they behave in an habitual fashion which does not entail any consideration of the rule.

It has been proposed that behaving in accordance with rules involves behaving for reasons. Schwayder, for instance, suggests that 'to conform to a rule is to act with a certain kind of reason'. That is, 'rules are reasons' (: 245–50). McIntyre also refers to rule-governed behaviour as acting for reasons rather than causes. Now if we accept the earlier distinction between reflective and reflexive relationships to the rule, then it follows that only in instances of the former type could there conceivably be any connection between rules and reasons. This is not to suggest the reflexive behaviours are not rule-governed, but merely they cannot be linked to particular reasons. It only obscures the relationship between an individual and a rule to speak of a rule as being a kind of reason, for the absence of any one-to-one relationship between rules and reasons for following rules argues against any identification of one with the other. More properly, it should be suggested that people may have one of a variety of reasons, and possibly no reason at all, for conforming to a rule. As far as a person's relationship to a rule—or, better still, to the behaviour prescribed by the rule—is concerned, it seems likely that reflective relationships precede reflexive ones. In many instances people probably begin by consulting the rule and then come to follow it habitually. They come to obey the rule without choosing; in Wittgenstein's words they come to 'obey the rule blindly' (1953 : 85). This two-stage process may be exemplified in the way in which one acquires mastery of a second language.[4]

Earlier on we noted that people who know the rules may have various reasons for not following the rule. Likewise, we can now conclude that they may have various reasons for following the rule. Someone who follows the rule may believe that what it prescribes is in some sense morally good. Alternatively, he may be indifferent to its

---

4. This would not account for the way in which the child acquires a first language; if anything, the process is probably reversed. First language learning also poses another problem: in terms of the criteria we have established for attributing knowledge of a rule, the child could not be said to have acquired language until he is capable of either articulating certain critical linguistic rules or showing that he recognises where they have been broken.

ramifications or he may actually disapprove of the rule while following it for reasons of expediency. There is yet another argument why rules should not be confused with reasons. It should be evident that however much we studied, say, the rules of chess, we would not be able to understand what players try to do, nor would we be able to predict the course of any game. The rules of chess do not specify the end that people play to, just as they do not dictate what pieces should be moved. Instead, they simply limit what may be done; they provide a set of behavioural constraints within which motives may be realised. Beyond this, it is the purpose and the plan or strategy of the player that will determine his moves, and the alternation of these moves and those of his opponent that will determine the outcome of a game. So it is only through an analysis of goals and stratagems, *as these are contained by rules*, that one may come to understand a game of chess. Perhaps social behaviour is, in this sense, somewhat like a game of chess. In which case a mere explication of the rules will be insufficient to describe why people behave as they do. In order to explain their behaviour one would need to understand what they intend to accomplish, and how they work within the rules to achieve these ends. Only then could one begin to consider how it is that people use the rules to legitimise their actions and how they excuse themselves by reference to the rules.

So far the picture is not too complicated. We have accepted that whenever someone who knows a rule behaves in accordance with that rule, then his behaviour may be said to be rule-governed. This is in line with one of Winch's points. Winch has suggested that where someone displays an ability to distinguish between a right and a wrong way of doing things, it makes sense to say that he is applying a criterion in what he does (1971 : 55). Unfortunately for both Winch and ourselves, this is not necessarily the case. It is possible that under certain circumstances a person who knows the rules may engage in behaviour which cannot be referred back to the operation of that rule. Consider the chess player. Imagine that he has full knowledge of the rules of the game and that he and his opponent are playing on one of those modern chess boards where the pieces are unfamiliar and therefore relatively difficult to distinguish from one another. Suppose now that our player momentarily mistakes his queen for his king and that he moves the piece which he takes to be his king to an adjacent square. In moving his queen he would have had in mind the rule relating to movements of the king, although the actual move he made was permissible for both the king and queen. Here we have an instance where someone knows a rule and where his behaviour appears to be guided by that rule while it is in fact guided by another. Earlier on we noted that when people who are ignorant of a rule conform to that rule, then we are obliged to regard their behaviour as rule-fitting rather than rule-guided. Similarly, we can now see that even when someone knows the rule there may be instances where his behaviour, while it conforms to the rule, is actually guided by another rule or possibly even a reason which is wholly independent of any rule.

This leads us to the question of how an individual's knowledge of certain rules might govern his behaviour, and to the question of whether such rules are in fact the rules he consults in his appraisal of his own actions and those of other people. But let us consider each of these separately. We have observed that although someone might be shown to know a rule we cannot necessarily conclude that those of his actions which fit with that rule are guided by it; we cannot assume, just because someone applies a rule in his assessment of actions, that this rule in any way generates those actions of his which accord with the rule on other occasions. What remains then of the supposed sym-metrical property of a rule? It is often suggested that rules function both in the appraisal and generation of behaviour, but we have already noted that many rules are merely descriptive of appraisals and not behaviours. Conversely, we might add that there may be rules which are descriptive of behaviours but not appraisals. For example, we argued earlier that only those actions which satisfy the conditions of arbitrariness and/or breach may be regarded as candidates for explana-tion in terms of rules, and that those behaviours which fail to meet either of these criteria should be considered in terms of other kinds of explanation. At the same time we suggested, perhaps a little boldly, that knowledge of a rule be inferred from an individual's manifest ability to distinguish a right from wrong way of doing things. Taken together, these two proposals raise the possibility of an interesting anomaly which can best be illustrated by what happens on the pave-ment. When walking down the street English pedestrians commonly keep to the right side of the pavement (Collett and Marsh, 1974). The fact that there are people, in particular Australians and New Zealanders, who have the opposite habit of walking on the left suggests that pavement streaming exhibits the characteristics of a convention. In other words, we have a piece of behaviour which, because it satisfies the conditions of arbitrariness and breach, admits explanation in terms of a rule. However—and here is the rub—were we to, say, expose a group of English subjects to two clips of film, one depicting the English and the other the antipodean pavement convention, we would be extremely unlikely to elicit offended cries of 'wrong' or 'inappropriate' from our subjects, if in fact we were able to evoke any recognition of difference at all. What I am suggesting, then, is that there may be behaviours which allow for explanation in terms of rules but which are not reflected in people's appraisals of those behaviours. If it is the case that there are rules which are descriptive of behaviours or appraisals, but not both, then it follows that the idea of a rule as mediating between the actor as behaver and the actor as appraisor needs to be carefully reconsidered. In respect of language, for example, it may well be that the speaker and the hearer are not, at least in terms of rules, the same kind of animal.

Throughout our discussion we have emphasised that any attempt to uncover the rules that an individual knows should proceed from an examination of his intuitions concerning what counts as admissible behaviour and what does not. This implies that we will not accept formal codifications of rules, such as may be found in books on grammar or manuals on etiquette, as containing those rules which people either know or uphold. While the opinions of the recognised expert or a representative member of a community may provide useful clues as to the conceptions that prevail in a community, they will not necessarily indicate what people believe to be inappropriate behaviours. In short, we cannot accept, as does Lewis, that when an informant speaks for himself he also speaks for others. Even accepting that we only attribute knowledge of a rule on the basis of an ability to distinguish a right from wrong ways of behaving, we still have to confront the issue of what we mean and, more importantly, our informants understand by 'right' and 'wrong', or for that matter any one of the variety of criteria that have been used in this connection. Although expressions such as 'well-formed', 'acceptable', 'appropriate' and 'permissible' may appear on first inspection to be united by a central notion of 'correctness', the question of whether the application of different criteria discloses different features of an informant's social knowledge should not be allowed to go begging.

But what inferences can be drawn once we have established that our informant knows a rule? There is the assumption that if someone can be shown to know a particular rule then it naturally follows that he applies this rule in his appraisal of actions that are performed in situations similar to those in which the rule was elicited. Quite apart from the problem of what constitutes a comparable situation, there is also the question of whether the assumption is admissible. I suspect that it need not be, and that there will be cases where rules which have been uncovered under controlled eliciting conditions bear no resemblance to those that underlie someone's apparaisals outside those conditions. That is to say, we may discover that what people can do in our studies is not what they do elsewhere. In rugby there is a rule to the effect that the scrum half should place the ball in the scrum as soon as the opposing front rows have gone down, but it just so happens that scrum halves almost never follow the rule, and it could probably be shown that where they do act in a manner consistent with the rule they do so for strategic reasons rather than out of any concern for the rule. Furthermore, although a penalty is reserved for infringements of this scrummage rule it is seldom exercised by referees when the rule is broken. In other words, those who fall within the jurisdiction of this rule seldom follow it and are not usually penalised for their infractions. But more importantly this example raises the possibility of players either citing the scrummage rule or recognising instances of its breach while not regarding conformity to the rule as the 'proper' way of playing the game. If this is so in rugby then there may well be areas of social life which are characterised by discrepancies between prescribed and actual behaviours, and more to the point, between the rules that informants instanciate or recognise while in the solicitous company of the investigator and the rules that actually inform their appraisals on other occasions.

In summary, we have shown that the rule-concept is by no means a novel candidate in explanations of behaviour. We have discussed what it may mean to speak of someone as knowing a rule and have suggested that someone be attributed with knowledge of a rule only where he is capable of articulating the rule or where he exhibits an ability to apply the rule in evaluating behaviour. We have also drawn out the implications between knowing or not knowing a rule and behaving or not behaving in accordance with a rule and have referred to some of the problems associated with the concept. These notwithstanding, it seems that some concept or concepts of rule are bound to play a part in future accounts of social behaviour. This is not to suggest that we should be uncritical in our use of the idea, or that we should ever regard analyses in terms of rules as being in themselves sufficient explanations of social behaviour. In committing ourselves to the notion we will need to ensure that we are not tempted into believing that a periodic incantation of the term will, like some sympathetic magic, perform out science for us. We will need to ensure that we do not—to use Kuo's description of early instinct theory—produce a finished psychology.

Rules in the Explanation
of Social Behaviour

ROM HARRÉ

The problems facing us are as follows: First of all, why look for rules?
And second, what rules can we expect to identify as operative in social
life? I shall not concern myself with the deeper problem of the nature of
rules, simply assuming an intuitive understanding of the notion. We
shall seek rules both in the process of generation of social action, and in
its justification in the kind of talk we call 'accounting'. In our book,
Secord and I began from some general considerations of the nature of
psychology as a possible science and showed that the rule-following
idea led to a view of sociology roughly coincident with that of Goffman, and blended with certain aspects of ethnomethodology (Harré and
Secord, 1972). In this paper I shall proceed in the contrary direction and
try to show that a psychology which draws in an essential way on our
ordinary understanding of human action and literary and dramatic
sources is demanded by the idea of the social forms that are found in the
new sociology. To express the point of view of the new sociology, one
can manage with three central doctrines:

1.

A theory of the nature and natural course of development of institutions. An institution manifests itself in certain forms of orderliness in
people's behaviour and in the references they make to it in their
accounting. But what sort of being does it have? People certainly treat
institutions as if they were real. For example, many people are com-

pletely convinced of the existence of the University of Oxford, of the existence of various trade unions, clubs, nations, police forces, traffic schemes, etc. However, ethnomethodology teaches us to be very careful indeed in our assumptions about the mode of being of institutions and of social entities generally. It suggests that they have a conceptual rather than a concrete being. They exist, perhaps, in the way a grammatical construction exists. To say this is not to solve the problem of the mode of being of institutions but to align them with other entities of the same standing, so that we can draw upon our intuitions about entities whose surface appearance is somewhat less problematic.

The theory of the working and development of institutions I want to draw on in this paper is due to Goffman. In Goffman's theory, which you will find in *Asylums* (1970) and elsewhere, the underlying idea is that every institution takes on simultaneously two distinct forms. It can be seen as having two modes of organisation. It requires two systems of explanation for what happens within it. This duality arises because, as we would put it, the sense a person can make of what goes on in it, and what is happening to him, depends upon his ability to deploy two systems of rhetoric. An institution has an official theory which is used in official explanations of why it is there and what happens to people within it. It also has a dramaturgical theory. An institution, Goffman claims, not only exists to perform its official functions, but it also provides the staging for dramas of character. In certain kinds of institutions the dramaturgical aspect of the institution slowly comes to dominate the official one. Institutions pass through a natural history, from a condition explicable on the predominantly official theory, to a state which is intelligible only on an almost wholly dramaturgical theory. In the last state of an institution the official rhetoric may appear in descriptions of activities which, to an outsider, may appear as only symbolic, in mere ritual performances of its official tasks. A theory of the history of institutions could be elaborated which would explain, in terms of the demands people make of life, the passage from a condition intelligible wholly in terms of the official rhetoric to one largely explicable in dramaturgical terms. For example, the mediaeval Guilds, which were officially for the regulation of the behaviour of craftsmen in the City of London, gradually became predominantly dramaturgical institutions. I believe that trade unions are at present in an intermediate position. They have an official theory (they are supposed to be concerned with the improvement of the conditions of working people), but they have a very strong dramaturgical element in them and they partly now constitute stagings for dramas of personality and character.

Each point of view generates a rhetoric, by the use of which a person makes sense, both for himself and others, of what he finds himself doing. This is one of the central ethnomethodological ideas. One of the rhetorics will encapsulate the official view and one of the rhetorics will encapsulate the dramaturgical view.

The central problem with which an ordinary person is faced, in his social life, is how to make sense of his situation. It is the astonishing success that most people have in finding solutions to this problem which makes ethnomethodologists and other right-thinking people see most men and women as profoundly successful social psychologists and sociologists. Everyone is faced with the problem of finding explanations of the positions in which they find themselves. How does a woman explain her situation? She draws upon the theories that she knows in making sense of the situation in which she finds herself. If a Women's Libber, she may draw upon a political rhetoric. In an institution she may draw upon either an official rhetoric or the dramaturgical rhetoric in explaining what her situation is and what is going on around her. And different people in different situations in the same institution may draw on different rhetorics.

It is a very important principle, from our point of view, that all rhetorics have the same standing as the bases for scientific theories of the social behaviour of human beings. For *sub specie aeternitatis* as conceptual resources for describing and explaining what is really there, all rhetorics are as good as each other. There is no rhetoric which is in a privileged position as providing a true and complete description of what occurs in an institution. So the official theory of an institution, the dramaturgical theory, and however many other theories of an institution there are, with their associated rhetorics, are of equal standing from the point of view of their empirical truth and the partiality of their view. It is an important consequence of this view that the ordinary man's rhetoric, the social psychologist's and the sociologist's rhetoric, are just rhetorics among other rhetorics. There might be certain advantages in the adoption of one rather than another, but then again there might not.

2.

When one is examining the performance of an institution on its official side, we can say that what the institution consists of, amongst other things, is a set of rules. These could be written down, though usually only a few reach explicit formulation. These rules govern people's performance in carrying out the tasks laid down in the official rhetoric as well as defining and thus constituting the elements of the institution itself. Thus, relative to the official rhetoric, we have the notion of performance in an institution. Now, of course, when you are performing in an institution you are also engaged in a drama of character, putting people down, grabbing another step up in the status hierarchy, showing yourself off to the best advantage in front of members of the opposite sex, etc., etc.

But there are no written rules for guiding and judging one's performance in these matters. And yet there are acceptable and unacceptable ways of proceeding, and there are at least tacit conventions limiting the scope of behaviour in various ways. For the representation of this tacit knowledge we can extend the idea of a rule to include what we, as self-aware participants, taking the standpoint of an observer, would write down or otherwise formulate propositionally as the conventions operative in, say, how junior executives treat the girls in the typing pool.

3.

But while one is playing one's part in a drama of character, one has to be getting on with the official performance as well, even if in ritualised form. So how *can* there be dramaturgical performances in an institution where everybody is getting on with the official job? Let us say you are negotiating with an employer over a wage demand. How can you at the same time then be carrying on a drama of character? 'Character-work' is possible because when performing we act in accordance with a certain style, qualifying our actions by the manner in which we carry them out.

Duties are performed alright, but always with a certain style. The description of the performance will, generally speaking, appear in verbs, and descriptions of style will generally be manifested in adverbs. Wage claims can be negotiated churlishly, elegantly, cheerfully, disconsolately, etc. The adverbs represent the style, the verbs the performance. It is in the style of performance that the dramaturgical aspect of an institution is carried on. It is then that character is manifested and risked. I refer you to Goffman's studies of the many particular rhetorics and styles to be found in the by-play of institutions, a by-play which we are bold enough to say is their main reason for existing. We could call the rules which relate ways of doing things to their dramaturgical import, *maxims*. We shall speak of dramaturgical maxims in contrast to rules of performance.

What I have said so far could be held to be still within sociology. Of course, I am hinting here at the necessity of a psychological theory as to how a person *can* function in the ways we have seen he actually carries on in an institution.

To develop such a theory in detail it must be related to a theory of the human person which, to take a phrase from Harré and Secord, can be called an anthropomorphic theory of human beings. Let us take the desperate expedient of supposing that for scientific purposes human beings can be treated as if they were people. Our general theory of human nature will encapsulate that central idea. From an analysis of the notion of a person, we find that we require to dichotomise the functioning of a person with respect to his particular kind of behaviour. One of the things that one is very struck with about people, and quasi-people such as Washoe, and rudimentary people such as cats, is that we are much inclined to say in explaining what they are doing, that they know of certain things, they are aware of certain things, they take into account certain things, and so on: we use a certain kind of language which involves some measure of consciousness being ascribed to that entity, of course not necessarily in the course of our accounting for all of its actions, but certainly for some. And that is as much as to say that the entity is monitoring its performance, it is recording, and often watching over what it does. The cat's paw goes out, and there is a more or less complex feedback system in which the action is monitored and the form of action is controlled in accordance with the monitoring. According to the *ethogenic* theory (Harré and Secord, 1972), that is not enough to explain the things that human beings can do, even so simple a thing as picking up a piece of chalk, let alone the kind of things we have argued that people are characteristically doing in institutions. A second order of monitoring is required in which the details of the performance which is now being carried out, including even its end as conceived by the actor, are recorded. That is, the whole performance *and its representation within the organism,* is conceived of as an entity of which one can be aware. In that state one is *sometimes* aware of, and *always* recording, not just the mouse and the act of grabbing the mouse, but both the envisaged and the remembered hunt. To be able to do this we must be capable of second order monitoring. Because we engage in this kind of monitoring we have the information necessary to exercise second order control, and because we satisfy this requirement, we *can* perform according to a certain style. And, of course, Goffmanian sociology knows that, as a matter of fact, we do.

If it is the case that social personae are manifest in the style in which a person does a thing, and that style can be under the control of a person's consciousness in the way he carries on his performance, then of course we would expect there to be a multiplicity of personae available to a human being, a multiplicity of social personae which a person can produce, and his con-specifics can recognise. So there will not be just one social persona per human being; a multiplicity is possible. This fits with some work done under the old paradigm by Argyle and Little (1971), which can be rewritten in ethogenic terms, in which they showed that there were a multiplicity of personae displayed, each in a certain kind of social interaction, appropriately adjusted to the kind of situation in which each was displayed, and to its characteristic kind of behaviour.

I have already made the point that in considering action we want to consider action both as to what act is performed by what actions, i.e. what is the social meaning of that set of actions, and the manner or style in which it is performed. This will then be a theory of *social* action. It can be called an ethogenic theory because it is a theory of the genesis of social action as well as an analysis of the way people justify and explain what they do. This theory would hold that in a large class of cases social action is a kind of skilled action, but unlike the theory that Michael Argyle (1969) earlier espoused, under the spell of the ghost of behaviourism lingering in his laboratory, it is not like a *motor* skill. It is a kind of intellectual skill, i.e. it is exercised upon elements organised according to their meanings, and involves *not* sub-routines of the kind Bruner has recognised in motor skills, but rather intelligent appreciation of those meanings and their ramifications, and admits the possibility of their intelligent manipulation.

It is *because* social competence is an intellectual skill, i.e. can come under second order monitoring and control, that there can be such people as machiavellians, con men, actors and other professional prevaricators. A machiavellian is someone who deliberately, for a higher order end or intention, controls the style in which he performs in order to produce a persona which he actively desires to produce, which he sees as a performance upon the ground of a performance. Machiavellian action is possible because any man can raise the level of his self-awareness since as a human being he has been monitoring all levels of his actions, as can an actor, or a small child, or a con man, or Garfinkel's (1967) Agnes, or anyone whose attachment to his tasks and the style of their performance has not become wholly habitual and routine. It is because there is monitoring of style that it is possible for a person to control, deliberately, the style in which he or she performs, and thereby control his or her presented personae. Now it is *that* feature, really, which drives us towards a study of the role of rules, taken both literally and metaphorically, in the control, preparation and justification of action.

There is one last but crucial element in all this, looked at from the sociological side, which I must mention before I collect up the rule-talk in a systematic fashion. It is the fact that meaningful action involves other people. So far I have been talking from the point of view of the one, the central one, the person who is acting, and I have been looking at it from the point of view of he who wants to act, wants to do something, wants to do it in a certain style, wants to convince somebody that he is a certain kind of person, and so on. Now to act successfully in that way, the actor requires a realm of others who have a complementary set of skills, namely competence in understanding the actions of the other person as this or that kind of action, this or that kind of meaning representing this or that kind of person. This is really a very deep point since our very being as persons depends upon our meanings being available to others willing to read them. We are only people, that is, creatures whose actions are meaningful as acts, in so far as we can be recognised as such by our con-specifics. How can they do that?

According to the ethogenic critique of traditional empirical methods, there is an enormous theoretical dichotomy between two theories as to the way in which one human being can interact with another. There is the old S-R theory whose spectre still haunts psychological laboratories. People still imagine that in some way or another they can decompose the influence one human being has upon another into a variety of elementary stimuli which then call forth a variety of elementary responses, and somehow or another the totality of a socially meaningful situation is made up of the sum of socially meaningless elements. Now S–R was repudiated as an official theory of psychology a long time ago, but of course one of the things that Secord and I were able to show, I think quite successfully, was how much experimental work still assumes the truth of the analytical principles of that point of view.

For instance, one may partition day-to-day human interaction into, for example, such an elementary element as frequency of interaction. One might try to find out what degree of liking—if we are talking now of a social psychological experiment—is produced by frequency of interaction. One might try to find out the effect of some other elementary partitioned element of the presentation of one human being to another. This, mind you, is offered as an account of the factors involved in one human being coming to like another. Liking at the other end of the causal chain is similarly regarded as an elementary component of attitude. At best on the causal end, the elements offered by traditional experimental psychologists have a very striking characteristic. They are formal. They are such entities as repetition, as round or square shapes, amount of gaze, or whether or not the interlocutor is wearing spectacles. Frequently the elements are of the super-formal 'go' or 'no-go' character of formal logic. In the traditional 'experiment' the formal elements are then 'presented' one by one, and their alleged effects observed and similarly partitioned. Correlations between the elements are looked for in the old-fashioned experimental way. The set of formal elements or, as they are often misleadingly called, 'variables' on each side of the alleged productive relation is supposed to add up to a socially meaningful entity, e.g. something like the liking one person may have for another. So social interaction is supposed to take place through purely formal modes of action (see Zajonc, 1968).

Another example is the experiments on social facilitation, carried out by Zajonc (1965). Social facilitation is the effect that occurs when someone watching you makes you do a thing better (or worse). In the traditional way Zajonc partitioned the presence of another person into a set of formal elements, e.g. whether he is such-and-such a distance away from the other person, or in such an orientation, and then he tried to correlate the socially meaningful effect with changes in purely formal elements.

Some while ago Vygotsky (1936), in that magnificent book *Thought and Language*, pointed out that this was to commit a serious error which was both scientific and philosophical. When we are studying the interactions of social life we are dealing with an entity which has unitary social meaning as a whole and which we cannot partition into purely formal meaningless elements, take them separately and expect them to generate the elements of the same socially meaningful effect that was produced by the unpartitioned ensemble. One might say that the ensemble has a unitary semantic quality. The semantic quality of the presence of that entity to a knowledgeable perceiver is lost the moment it is partitioned into purely formal elements. Just as a finite number of zeros cannot make a finite interval, so too socially meaningless elements, taken separately, cannot add up to a socially meaningful ensemble. No number of formal entities is going to make up something which is semantically significant.

The semantic element is something which is in fact independent of any particular formal structure. In order to do social psychology, or any other social science for that matter, the social world must be partitioned or analysed into the minimal semantically meaningful elements. If it is the structural organisation of a whole face attached to a whole body that is a semantically meaningful element, then what interacts are whole people. It is easy to see this with a very simple example. Suppose I had written down 'the cat' and I wanted to translate it into another language. Now I might (following the remnant of the traditional S–R view still assumed in the laboratory experiment) partition it as follows: 't.h.e. + c.a.t.' and then I might have to try to find out a rule which transformed it letter by letter, hoping that the result of the transformation would be something in another language. But we know that won't work. Why? Because the partition I have made is into elements which are only formally present in the word. What I have to do is to identify the semantic elements. In Spanish it's very convenient since 'the' → 'el,' and 'cat' → 'gato', so there is no formal correspondence between the letters. Yet we can easily see that 'el gato' is a translation of 'the cat'. To look for a relationship between the letters would be an example of the kind of error someone would make if they failed to make the distinction between the formal and the semantic partition of meaningful entities. We want to insist upon the idea that the units of social analysis are through and through semantic. That is, we are interested primarily in the social meanings of physically differentiated elements and their semantic organisation; only secondarily in the physical differentia and their formal organisation. It is between social *meanings* that social laws, if there are any, hold and of which social patterns are made up. This poses a very interesting problem.

The moment we turn to meanings as the focus of investigation, the whole nature of psychological study is transformed. Personae are presentations of oneself under a meaningful aspect. If someone does not know the meaning of the stylistic qualifications of what I am doing, then they cannot see me under the aspect I intend to present. If someone does not understand the *meaning* of the distinction between short and long hair these days, though he will be able to see that someone's hair is long, he will be unable to see that he is radical, or fashion conscious, or whatever. He will not be able to follow the transformation of meaning of the formal distinction between long and short hair. We can perhaps think of five years ago when long hair did have some kind of political significance. Those who wore their hair long meant themselves to be seen as occupying a certain political stance and they were making this manifest by using the formal distinction between the short and long hair as having a certain semantic loading. Fortunately for this example, in the 1790s they also used the short and long hair distinction, but the semantic loading was exactly the other way round. The extreme left had their hair short, the extreme right had theirs long. Similarly, with the bra/no bra distinction. If you read advertisements when the brassière was introduced in the 1880s, these offered this garment as a blow for women's liberation. The brassière enabled them to cast away restrictive stays. It was offered as the great liberator. If you look at trendy magazines of four or five years ago the same rhetoric occurs, but exactly the opposite proposition is offered. The semantic loading is round the other way. Contradictory social meanings are borne by the formal distinction between A and no-A, in various physical embodiments, between short and long hair, loose clothes versus tight, etc. The physically differentiated structures are used to convey different semantic distinctions at different times. It is clear that the principles of social analysis must emphasise the primacy of the semantic and allow the formal only a secondary role; at least in cases like those I have cited. So, the rules for the use and understanding of formally differentiated structures are shot through with semantics. The psychology of man as a social being hovers on the borderline of semantics and syntax.

From a semantic point of view the items which appear in styles of behaviour, clothes and hair, in vocabulary of gesture, are mere bricolage. If there are semantic universals they will be found in patterns of meaning which, culturally, are relatively independent. But in each culture the common system of meanings is conveyed by a different physically differentiated system. It is upon this last that the social world actually operates. We will reserve the word 'conventions' for the rules which link the culturally idiosyncratic matters, i.e. gestures, with the socially universal meanings, e.g. goodbye. We shall speak of these as conventions of meaning.

Anything which can provide physically differentiable states can be the basis of a semantic system; and any physically differentiable states which are intimately involved in our lives are naturally candidates for meaning. For instance, those physiological states which leak through into consciousness and which we then call feelings are sufficiently intimate and sufficiently peremptory to be in need of interpretation, that is, to be endowed with meaning. But in the case of a feeling, there can be no question of intention. Thus, to give a feeling a meaning, is to locate it within a system, and thus to explain it. For instance, a feeling of nervous excitation might be given meaning as 'love' and thus located within a systematic framework of people, traditions, expectations and other meanings. An emotion is a feeling endowed with such meaning. And since the attribution of meaning is a theoretical exercise the very same feeling may appear as a quite different emotion if embedded in a different systematic context. It is clear that knowledge of possible contexts of this sort and of their structure is included in what we should call literary and artistic sources of social science.

It is one of the tasks of comparative social psychology to determine how far the relation between particular physically differentiated systems of bearers as vehicles and the meaning system they convey is arbitrary. That there is a large measure of arbitrariness is certain. This follows from the way the same physically differentiated states of the world are capable of conveying quite different social meanings, and from the fact that the same meanings may be conveyed by widely different physical vehicles. From what we already know, it looks as if the significance of the particular vehicular systems for the conveyance of meaning for psychology is almost negligible, alongside the possibility of universal structures of meaning.

The effect of taking the new sociology seriously can be summarised in the answers that can now be given to my two general questions.

Why Rules?

(i) Because for a certain class of behaviour people are monitoring both performance and style and they are capable of exercising some form of conscious control over both. People are actors as well as agents. (*ii*) Because the whole system of social actions is shot through with semantic loading, with meanings. And the idiosyncratic systems by which meanings are conveyed are cultural constructs, cultural entities. The only structures that look like being universal are the patterns of meanings. There may be some formal universals but they have not so far emerged. It is doubtful even if the smile and frown are so fixed in sense that they can be understood socially as simply muscle-movements. The most powerful concept for representing the way we are related to these action-systems and forms of control is the notion of rule, extended by metaphor to include the propositional representations of conventions which are effective in rudimentary cases by non-verbal means.

What Rules?

(*i*) There are rules governing the patterns of action, that is, which instruct us how actually to perform a certain task in the course of which presentation of the self may occur, but which is aimed at some other level of social action, perhaps the act which the doing of the action accomplishes. The system of such rules is built around such notions as roles, institutions, etc. (*ii*) There are rules for the presentation of selves, which we shall call 'maxims'. Amy Vanderbilt (1963) recommends that the host in paying the bill in a restaurant 'looks at it sufficiently long to see if there are errors but never so long and methodically as to make him seem niggardly' (: 586). There are many such maxims both more specific and more general according to which some from the range of acceptable selves are to be selected and presented, and by reference to which the presentation of an unattractive or morally objectionable persona can be avoided. (*iii*) Both the presentation of selves and the recognition of the self-presentation of others in the style of a performance, requires the recognition of the meanings of the culturally idiosyncratic symbolic system by which items of presentation and action are performed so as to be read by others. This kind of rule has to do with the assignment of meanings to gestures, grimaces, verbal formulae, etc. We call them 'conventions'.

As I emphasised earlier, the notion of rule is not intended to be taken with absolute literalness in all contexts. We are using the notion of rules for building models of cognitive processes which may not be available to consciousness (Mischel, 1975).

One important proviso: I have said that Secord and I and others have felt ourselves obliged to repudiate explicitly the idea that *all* social patterning is to be explained by reference to rules. There might be items other than rules involved as formal causes, structured templates of action. We do believe, of course, that a very large class of patterned sequences of action is explicable by reference to the above categories of rules. But there might be some cases where it is literally not true that there are rules or rule-like structured templates responsible for the patterning of manifest action-sequences, and where the processes which lead to these patterns are not cognitive in any sense. Suppose, for example, that it were the case that every society we examine organised itself according to a hierarchical system. Its people arrange themselves pyramidally, sometimes literally as in a throne room, sometimes metaphorically as in some elaborate, graded system of honorific titles. Of course, these hierarchical systems would have very different semantic loadings in different societies and a very great variety of different rhetorics with the help of which the local society explains to itself why the hierarchy had to be. It might be that there is something which drives human beings towards this kind of organisation, just as there is something which drives human beings towards structuring their language according to the subject-predicate distinction. We would be unwise to insist, with Chomsky, if there are such formal universals, that they must be built into the physiological system, since they may derive from very fundamental but pervasive features of human life, such as there being two sexes, that parents are bigger than their children for a while, and so on.

We regard it as absolutely crucial to determine which elements in the generation of social patterning are derivative from universal formal relationships and which are semantic universals, as it is quite clear that for the purposes of social technology there is all the difference in the world between them. If the patterning is to be explained as the product of a semantically operative cultural system which is learned in the course of the cultural development of an individual, then of course that is up for possible change by the appropriate social technology, if one could find out what it was. But if the universal feature is embedded in certain fundamental or physiological aspects of human life, then of course it is not up for possible change without drastic evolutionary development. Now it seems to me that it is a matter of crucial importance to social psychologists to get on to this problem, to try to distinguish between those cases where we really are dealing with an inbuilt or otherwise unchangeable structural universal and cases where we are dealing with cultural and semantic entities, determining behaviour through the effectiveness of rules. With the kind of experiment that is still going on nobody is ever going to find this out, because they commit Vygotsky's fallacy right from the start, confusing human relations mediated by meanings with those mediated by automatic processes beyond the control of the individual or the modulations brought about by changes in society. Such investigators will discern meaning units only by accident, or by unthinking projection of their own meaning systems upon the social world, e.g. as revealed in Moscovici's (1972) strictures upon the social psychology of 'nice guys'. One must ask oneself, 'What are the semantic units and how do they acquire their social meaning?', seeing one's own attribution of meaning as problematic, that is, as requiring analysis and explanation.

The new study of comparative primate social psychology, when finally wrested from the hands of the journalists, ought to be very illuminating. If we find in our nearest brethren, hairy little people like Washoe, that she and her con-specifics organise their lives upon similar formal structures to ourselves, we will have very strong grounds for supposing that the universals we have identified in this case are indeed genetically or, in some other way, biologically based and therefore non-negotiable (see Gardner and Gardner, 1968).

So I shall also assert that in addition to wanting social psychologists to pursue the rule and social semantics line in a search for universal meaning structures, I also think we need to do a lot more hard work on comparative social psychology between non-human primates and ourselves, and of course, happily, this kind of thing is now beginning. That should be pursued, in pursuit of exactly the same kind of question, namely to distinguish the formal from the semantic, the biological from the cultural. That is why I think we must use the concept of rule in our studies. That is the kind of control and genesis of patterns of human action I believe are central, and these are the rules there probably will turn out to be.

Rules and Sequences in Conversation

DAVID D. CLARKE

Human social interaction consists of more than just a collection of events selected at random from the actor's behavioural repertoire. It is a highly structured activity. That being the case it should be possible to detect the patterns of activity which characterise interactions and to infer from them the generative processes which govern the actor's behavioural output. Several aspects of the actor's behavioural pattern could be used in this way, including the non-random distribution of behavioural items in space, in time and over persons, but one kind of pattern seems to offer a unique opportunity for the study of psychological processes and that is the temporal order of behavioural events. As J.S. Mill (1851 : 335) put it:

> Of all truths relating to phenomena, the most valuable to us are those which relate to the order of their succession. On a knowledge of these is founded every reasonable anticipation of future facts, and whatever power we possess of influencing those facts to our advantage.

In social psychology the succession of events has a special importance for the following reason. The brain is a device for seeking, storing and processing information which it receives by way of sensory nerves, and to which it responds by way of the motor nerves. It confers an evolutionary advantage on the species because of the way it relates items of outgoing information to each other, and to previous items of incoming information. In short, it allows the organism to engage in complex coordinated activities, selected with respect to the properties of the environment, and hence to stay alive. Consequently the properties of the brain are well represented in the contingency of response upon stimulation, and it is this relation which has been the principal concern of most experimental psychologists. The way in which each piece of stimulus information evokes a response is of natural concern to anyone interested in the brain, but the way in which the organism's response influences future stimuli depends on the physical properties of the environment, and that is of little psychological interest. So there is a temptation when dealing with the psychology of the invidivual to look only for those relations which exist between one stimulus and one response, or at best the structure of a very short segment of stimulus-response recording.

In social interaction the position is different. Each member of a dyad, for example, produces responses which relate to previous stimuli, but in their turn they act as stimuli for the other person, whose responses are stimuli for the first. In this way a communicative cycle is established, in which the succession of events, which all appear to the outside observer as responses by some actor or other, is entirely governed by the stimulus-response and response-responses contingencies of the individuals. Thus the behaviour stream is governed by and embodies just those qualities of the actors which are of greatest psychological interest. The behavioural record can now be represented as a succession of events by one actor or another, rather than as distinct stimuli and responses, and treated to the sequential analyses devised for use in other disciplines such as linguistics and ethology.

The working of a behaviour-generating device can be described in several ways. One kind of description involves the mechanical properties of the device, such as the anatomy and physiology of the brain, or the electronic circuitry of a computer. This might be called a *hardware* description. In contrast there are the varieties of *software* description which deal with the information which is processed and the derivation of one string of symbols from another. Such a description may be couched in the form of a set of generative rules which produce all and only the outputs of the device, or the class of outputs of which it is potentially capable. It must be emphasised of course that the production of a realistic output by a set of generative rules in a psychological study does not necessarily imply that the actor's brain employs those same operations, but in so far as their outputs are identical the rules and the cerebral operations must embody equivalent information. That

information which is common to the brain and the generative rules
which mimic its capacities is usually referred to as *competence*, while the
particular use to which the knowledge is put and the real mental
operations involved belong to the realm of *performance* (after Chomsky,
1965).

Let us consider the competence component of a software description
of the generation of social behaviour sequences as opposed to accounts
of performance or hardware. That choice, though controversial, has the
advantages of offering an account of behavioural phenomena at a
level of description which is closer to our everyday encounters with
behavioural patterns, problems and solutions than is yet possible with
neurological descriptions. At the same time it offers a simpler and more
manageable picture of the behaviour stream than the study of performance, which must necessarily account for competence *and* a number of
other complex determinants of behavioural output. This is why the
study of speaker's or actor's knowledge of social and communicative
systems has been popular with so many linguists and anthropologists.
So far the discussion has concerned social behaviour in general. We
should now turn to one particular aspect of interaction, namely the
verbal components of conversation, to illustrate the point in greater
detail, bearing in mind that some of the following points could be
applied to the analysis of non-verbal behaviour as well.

The analysis of sequences of communicative events is perhaps best
exemplified by linguistics, and it is in the linguistic literature that many
of the following terms and concepts are to be found. Chomsky (1957,
1965) offers a particularly useful model for the sequential structure of
communicative acts, and his terminology will be used to describe some
of the more interesting properties of the stream of social behaviour,
which we might seek to validate in empirical studies.

The first thing one needs to know about a temporally structured
message, interaction or code is the pattern to which the output strings
conform. This will be called *surface structure*. To describe the surface
structure of the behaviour stream one must be able to perform three
operations. First, the ongoing flow of behaviour must be partitioned
to give discrete behavioural events, and the means of partitioning
should conform to adequate criteria of reliability and appropriateness.
Then the events which are detected in this way must be classified. This
is a crucial step, since some forms of social behaviour rarely, if ever,
recur. What does recur is the orderly progression of behavioural types,
rather than an orderly progression of the behaviours themselves.

When the behaviour stream is viewed as a succession of such behavioural types, the sequential patterns and interrelations may be recorded. That concludes the description of surface structure. Three further issues then arise. One is the relation of the form of a sequence to its meaning or interpretation. This might be called the issue of behavioural semantics and it raises the possibility that a semantic representation or *deep structure* will be required in the description of the behaviour stream which does not necessarily stand in one-to-one correspondence to the surface structure. Furthermore, if we should find that the surface structure of social interaction gives an accurate representation of performance, it could help us to determine the actual generative processes which lead the actor to behave as he does, and perhaps enable us to predict and influence behaviour in real-world settings.

In the remaining sections these issues will be considered according to the following plan: surface structure will be dealt with under the three headings of partitioning, categorisation, and sequence analysis; while deep structure and generative processes will occupy a further section.

Surface Structure

Partitioning The division of the behaviour stream into discrete particles, units or events is the first stage of sequential analysis. It might be achieved reliably by marking points of apparent discontinuity in the ongoing activity without necessarily capturing the functional boundaries between the elements of the system. There would then be a danger that the subsequent stages of analysis would be based upon an invalid partitioning and therefore be largely inaccurate. In the English language, for example, the phonological structure often shows more notable minima in sound energy within than between words, so an attempt to identify the principal units with discrete bursts of sound energy would be misleading.

The idea of a structure composed of units usually implies that there is a variable structural integrity in the system which is greatest within units and somewhat less between them. This shows up in the way that a structured object fractures. The principal units tend to remain intact while the object divides at unit boundaries. The process of identifying units by stressing the structure to observe the points of cleavage might be called partitioning by fragmentation. There is also a second approach. Some objects, though built up from basic units, are held together by bonding forces which are stronger than the original pieces. Such objects do not break at the boundaries between the pieces from which they were originally composed. Such pieces could only be detected using a process of partitioning by aggregation, in which small units were assembled, and the tendency of certain combinations to recur was used as the diagnostic feature of principal units. In the case of the sequential analysis of events this now illustrates one of the major complications. The three analytic stages of partitioning, classifying and sequencing which were previously presented as independent, are not completely independent after all. Units may be detected by reference to recurring sequences as we have just seen, and classification is even more dependent on sequence analysis, but sequence analysis in its turn depends on partitioning and categorisation. In practice the analysis cannot proceed from the completion of one stage to the beginning of the next, but only by revisiting and rechecking each stage against the others in successive iterations.

Most of the experimental studies which have been done on the partitioning of behaviour have used techniques of fragmentation rather than aggregation. One way of stressing the behaviour stream to see where it breaks is by interrupting the subject's production or perception of a string (bearing in mind that these two alternatives may give different results). Perhaps the most famous use of such a technique is to be found in the 'click' experiments on the syntactic units (e.g. Fodor and Bever, 1965). It was found that clicks played to subjects in the vicinity of a phrase boundary in a sentence they were listening to were recalled as closer to the phrase boundary than they had actually been. This suggests that in organising the linguistic input into chunks for analysis, and consequently in perceiving other events as occurring between the linguistic ones, the subjects had been using the same units of linguistic analysis as syntactic theories would suggest. In an experiment on the interrupted output of sentences, Yngve (1973) found that subjects, interrupted in mid-sentence by the intrusion of a secondary task, tended to resume their speech in an interesting way. They would go back to the beginning of the clause they had been on when interrupted, recapitulate up to the point of interruption, go on and finish that clause successfully, and then forget what they had been going to say. This elegant procedure provides a way of identifying the units in which material is transcribed into a different form of store prior to being output. Argyle (1975 : 64) found that subjects who had to judge tape recordings of speakers being interrupted, found the interruption most acceptable when it occurred at the end of a sentence, less so at the end of a clause, and least appropriate in mid-clause.

In a different kind of experiment on the psychological reality of syntactic descriptions, Johnson (1965) used memory as the means of indicating breaks in the behaviour stream. He asked subjects to recall sentences they had learned, and he recorded the transitional error probabilities at each point in the sentences (the probabilities that each word would be wrong given that the previous word was recalled correctly). These transitional error probabilities were found to be greatest at grammatical phrase boundaries.

Unit boundaries may be detected by the simpler procedure of asking subjects to mark what they believe to be event boundaries, when presented with a representation of the behaviour stream. Dickman (1963) showed filmed sequences of activity to subjects and then presented the same events as a set of cards each representing a small part of the film. The subjects sorted the cards into piles, each pile representing a segment of the activity on the film. A clearly hierarchical structure emerged, with some gross boundaries apparent to all subjects, while others were only recognised by those subjects who were apparently operating on a lower criterion of judgement since they produced more units. It was not the case that the subjects who only recognised a few boundaries, found boundaries which went unrecognised by those subjects who identified more. The level of judgement at which a subject identifies event boundaries may also influence and be influenced by other factors in the situation. Newtson (1973) showed video-tapes of social interactions to his subjects in one of two conditions in which they were asked to attend to fine or coarse units and mark them by activating an event recorder. He found that the attributions made to the actors by subjects instructed to mark fine boundaries were relatively more differentiated, more confident and more dispositional.

The various techniques which may be used to partition a behaviour stream are of great importance when studying some kinds of activity. The structure of conversation, however, is relatively easy to partition without recourse to elaborate techniques of analysis. The real problems set in when we turn to the next stage of analysis in which units are categorised.

Categorisation The detection of sequential patterns in social behaviour, as in anything else, depends on the recurrence of strings of events. The problem is that most events seldom recur, let alone the sequences they form. It is most uncommon for a particular combination of actor, setting and action to be repeated and if one includes the time of occurrence in the definition of an event, then a repetition becomes impossible. What does recur is not the events themselves but the classes of event. For example A might meet B one morning and say 'How did the week-end go, did you get to the Lakes in the end?' to which B replies 'No, the weather looked too bad on Friday so we stayed to paint the bathroom.' It is most unlikely that that exchange will ever occur again, particularly between those people and in that place. If the behaviour is recorded for analysis in some form which gives a unique coding to that particular form of words, then a recurring pattern is unlikely to emerge. If, however, the exchange is coded *Greeting, Question, Answer* or *Greeting, Request for News, News* or something similar, then recurrent patterns may emerge. That is all very obvious. Less obvious are the dangers of using an arbitrary (although possibly quite reliable) system for assigning events to categories. This is the point at which most attempts at a sequence analysis run into difficulties. The final statement that the observed form of events has a certain pattern can only really mean that a number of quite distinct behaviour sequences have been classified as being similar by the investigator. If the classification is ill founded then the whole analysis is void.

One must remember when drawing up an event taxonomy that it is to be used for a particular purpose, namely the description of behaviour sequences, and that some aspects of behaviour have no direct bearing on the formation of such sequences. The use of these features as the basis for a taxonomy would be most misleading. Suppose the problem were to write a grammar for a completely strange language. One would have to classify the words, and there would be a temptation to base that classification on those word properties which were obvious, operationally definable, and required no knowledge of semantics, such as length and phonetic structure. But then the language might turn out to work like English, and have a syntax which was not based on word length, together with annoying combinations of word properties, such as phonetic identity between words which are syntactically distinct and syntactic equivalence between words which are phonetically dissimilar. In such a case the correct assignment of words to classes could only be made if semantic information were available, and semantic information is not easily inferred by observation of performance. This suggests that the study of conversation sequences should proceed by *emic* methods in which the judgements of the native actor are employed, as opposed to *etic* methods based entirely on observation and inference (Pike, 1967).

It seems likely that the structurally important units of social behaviour will be distinguished by their semantic features rather than by their physical characteristics. Just as syntactic categories are defined by similarities of word meaning and function, but not necessarily of word sound, so too the most useful behavioural categories are likely to be based on similarities of perceived meaning rather than on the similarities between the particular forms of movement and speech in which social action is realised. That is not to say that each segment of the behaviour stream makes a single invariant contribution to the perception of meaning. Nor is it to suggest that one can simply convert each unit of form to a unit of content in order to have material which is suitable for sequential analysis, or in some other way representative of the meaning of the sequence of events. Such an assumption would be mistaken in two respects. Firstly, because the meaning of a behavioural item does not remain invariant regardless of the context in which it occurs, and secondly because there is a much more complex mapping than that between the semantic representation of a string and the sum total of the semantic features of its component parts. This is particularly true of elliptical remarks such as 'No' or 'Possibly' which affect the interpretation of a discourse in ways which depend on their context, and whose implications are more elaborate than an inspection of the words themselves might suggest.

If we accept then that a classification of events is a prerequisite for structural analysis, and that the classification must in some way take account of the meaning of the events rather than just their physical form, then we shall need some way of representing the similarities and differences between the semantic representations of events. One way of doing this would be to assign to each event a number of qualities or properties, each of which was present to a greater or lesser degree. One could conceive of the properties as a number of orthogonal dimensions, forming a space which represents the universe of possible behavioural events. Each point in the space would represent an event or type of event. There are several techniques of multivariate analysis which would produce such a representation from measurements of the attributes of a number of events or objects. They are largely unsuitable for the present purpose because the model of behaviour as the product of quasi-syntactic rules is based on the notion of sets of events and relations between sets, and therefore requires a categorical description of the event types. This also seems more suitable on psychological grounds since speech acts are likely to be subject, like most events, to categorical perception. That is to say, the events may be equally spaced along a physical continuum but they will be perceived as falling into discrete categories between which reliable discriminations may be made, but within which they are impossible. Liberman et al. (1957) found this to be true of English phonemes. When, for example, they played their subjects a range of auditory stimuli, synthesised so as to represent a range of possibilities from the phoneme /d/ to the phoneme /g/, the subjects tended to judge stimuli in part of the range as indistinguishable instances of /d/ and those in another part as indistinguishable instances of /g/.

If speech and social acts are subject to categorical perception, then it is all the more important to study them from an emic viewpoint, since the distinctions which are apparent to the actor and which influence his performance will not necessarily have counterparts in the domain of observable stimulus variations.

The events which make up the behaviour stream may be classified by identifying the equivalence relations between them. An equivalence relation is any relation which is reflexive, symmetric and transitive. Such a relation enables the events to be cast into a number of special sets called equivalence classes, which form a partition of the universe of events and which are each members of a quotient set. The union between all equivalence classes is the universe of behaviours, and the intersection of any two classes is ϕ, the empty set.

The particular relation which enables the event classes to be used in a subsequent sequence analysis is the relation of *having the same permissible occasions of use as*. If an event A has the same permissible occasions of use as an event B, and B has the same occasions of use as C, then A shares all occasions of use with itself (the relation is reflexive), B shares all occasions of use with A (the relation is symmetric) and A shares all occasions of use with C (it is transitive). In addition to having the properties of an equivalence relation and forming a partition of the set of possible events, this relation guarantees that the particular partition formed will optimise the quotient set, as a set of suitable event types for sequence analysis.

Saussure (1916) wrote of the structure of language as being characterised by two kinds of relations: *associative relations* (which have since come to be known as *paradigmatic relations*) and *syntagmatic relations*. The former exist between similar words (in derivation, meaning or syntactic class for example) while the latter exist between words which combine to form well-formed strings. Thus in the sentences

The glass is on the table.

and

The chair is on the floor.

paradigmatic relations could be said to exist between *glass* and *chair*, and *table* and *floor*, while syntagmatic relations could be said to exist between *glass* and *is*, and between *is* and *on*. An important doctrine of Saussure's was that syntagmatic and paradigmatic relations were inter-dependent and mutually defining. This property must be preserved in the linguistic analysis of behaviour sequences. Categories of behavioural events must be discovered by analysis of sequences, to find those events which can substitute for one another in any context. Only then can the classes so constituted be used to describe the common properties of all possible sequences within the system.

There is a technique for achieving this known as test frame analysis (Fries, 1952). A number of well-formed strings each have a single item deleted to form a test frame. Other items are substituted into the space left by the deletion, and a record is kept of all the items which can be inserted in a particular frame without destroying its structural integrity or well-formedness. Each set of mutually interchangeable items becomes a potential behavioural class, and it is to be hoped that the technique will yield a manageable number of classes which are mutually exclusive. This procedure has been applied to a number of hypothetical dialogues (Clarke, 1975) with the following result. No clear system of categories emerged, and the dendrogram which was used to represent the relations between individual items showed one large cluster, to which more and more individual items accrued, as the similarity criterion was relaxed. The reason for this was almost certainly that the units being classified were particular utterances, and these do not retain a stable function as they are moved from one context to another, as words do. An utterance like

'It's three o'clock'

could be seen as a statement, a reproach, a command or a number of other things depending on the context in which it was used, whereas a word like *carpet*, or *wall* or *sky* has the same syntactic function wherever it occurs. Of course there are exceptions, such as the word *smile* which can be a noun or verb, but it is generally true that the paradigmatic structure of sentences can be identified with the correspondence between particular words and particular syntactic classes, whereas in the analysis of discourse one must identify particular forms of words *as used in particular contexts* with their equivalence classes.

Searle (1965) has distinguished two kinds of rule that are found in the description of languages and games. Constitutive rules assign objects or events to classes and have the form *X counts as Y*. In a way, then, they generate paradigmatic structures. On the other hand regulative rules govern the use of the event classes, and have the form *If X, do Y*. The difference described above between the paradigmatic structures of language and discourse could be put another way by saying that the constitutive rules of languages are (largely) independent of context, while the constitutive rules for discourse and other forms of social behaviour are context dependent.[1]

Austin (1962) provides a particularly useful example of the way in which utterances can be categorised according to their social function. He was concerned to show that the traditional approach to semantics dealing with the propositional content of utterances as evaluated by their truth or falsity was incomplete. He suggested a second *performative* quality to be evaluated by the felicity or infelicity of the utterance (roughly success or failure) in achieving a particular function. The performative qualities of utterances include such things as threatening, advising, warning, persuading, and so on. These appear to be the kind of behavioural events which would feature in a meaningful sequence analysis, rather than the description of exact forms of words or movements. Austin further divided performatives into *illocutionary* and *perlocutionary* components. The illocutionary aspects of an utterance are those things achieved *in* saying it, while the perlocutionary aspects may be brought about *by* saying it. The distinction may be seen between the acts of urging and persuading. If I say 'Read this article to the end' then I have urged you to do something simply by the saying (or writing) of that utterance, and regardless of your response. On the

---

1. There are a large number of behavioural classifications in the literature of social psychology and human ethology, covering taxonomic procedures and the resulting taxonomies; verbal and non-verbal behaviours; categorical and dimensional models; acts and actions; different levels of linguistic description, and so on. It is not the purpose of this paper to review the work which has been done on behavioural categories and sequences, but to draw and illustrate certain conceptual and methodological points.

other hand to have *persuaded* you to read the entire article, I would have to have brought about some action on your part. The former is an instance of illocution and the latter of perlocution. Austin's further subdivision of performative utterances into five types does not meet the present requirements for an utterance taxonomy, but it does seem that the acceptable taxonomy will work at this level of linguistic description. That is to say, it will be a classification of performative types. As such, it could also be extended to include non-verbal events, since acts like threatening, rewarding, reproaching and so forth, can be performed verbally or non-verbally.

A more detailed examination of the paradigmatic structure of interpersonal events may be found in Osgood (1968, 1970). He considered a number of inter-personal verbs (IPVs) taken from *Roget's Thesaurus*. These are verbs expressing 'interpersonal intention', such as *to punish*, but not forms of activity such as *to strike with a whip*. The verbs were classified on a number of *a priori* features such as associative/dissociative and initiating/reacting. The codings were then checked to see whether similarly coded words really had similar meanings, and whether codings which differed in one respect only were an accurate reflection of differences in meaning. On the basis of these checks a different and more elaborate feature system was proposed. Osgood also used factor and cluster analytic methods to establish the relation between different IPVs. Small semantic frames were used to detect certain features of the IPVs. The frame, 'He . . . successfully', for example, can only incorporate words associated with goal achievement without becoming semantically anomalous. Again these studies do not provide the exact taxonomy required for a sequence analysis of verbal events, as they were not undertaken with sequential analysis in mind, and do not relate IPV classes to syntagms. The methods used do, however, look most promising for the taxonomic phase of a sequence analysis of conversations and social behaviour strings.

Van Hooff (1973) has described an elaborate study of the structure of chimpanzee social behaviour, which employed a technique for relating 'paradigms' and 'syntagms' (although he did not use these terms). A very fine behavioural classification was used to record behaviour sequences, which were then represented as a matrix of transitional frequencies. The number of times each item of behaviour was succeeded by each other item was entered in the matrix. The correlation between matrix entries for pairs of items was then used as the measure of inter-item similarity in subsequent factor and cluster analyses. This means that the criterion of similarity between items which is used in drawing up superordinate classes (the paradigmatic structure) is their similarity of occasions of use (their similarity of occurence in the syntagmatic structure). This technique has also been used to establish the paradigmatic relations between speech act types, on the basis of their use in sequences (Clarke, 1975).

Three problems arise at this stage of a structural analysis of social behaviour. The first has already been mentioned. It is that the constitutive rules by which items are assigned to equivalence classes are context dependent. Consequently the equivalence classes cannot be discovered by considering the utterances without reference to their contexts of use, nor can they be defined by instanciation, unless given forms of words are listed together with the definition of the contexts in which they function as a speech act of a particular type. Secondly, the assignment of events to classes may differ from individual to individual. This should not be too problematic, since in any working communication system, a consensus of judgement may be expected between participants. A third and more troublesome difficulty is that constitutive rules may vary from one situation to another. Certain categories of social event only exist in certain situations, while other more ubiquitous events may take on different realisations in different situations.

No one has yet overcome all these problems, to my knowledge, and arrived at a social event taxonomy meeting the requirements set out here, but perhaps it will not be long before a workable taxonomy is available which could be applied in the analysis of behaviour sequences.

Sequence analysis The orderly nature of language and social behaviour appears in a number of guises. It is shown by the pattern of speech as people use language in everyday life; it is shown by the knowledge that speakers have of the language which enables them to speak and understand it; and it could be said to be part of the object, Language itself, in so far as it is independent of the particular items of use and knowledge in which it is represented. These three things are usually treated by linguists as separate objects of study. The first was called *performance* by Chomsky (1965), in distinction to the second which he called *competence*. The first is also like Saussure's concept of *parole*, which he contrasted with the third which he called *langue*. One could make a similar distinction between the possible manifestations of social structure. The competence/performance distinction is particularly useful in the study of behavioural regularities. It should be appreciated, however, that while competence and performance correspond to some degree, it is not necessarily the case that those strings which are judged to be acceptable in a study of competence will be found to occur in a study of performance, or vice versa. Furthermore, the fact that competence can often be embodied in a series of generative rules, which will produce all and only the strings which are judged to be acceptable, does not imply that the generative operations of the rule system necessarily correspond to the generative process of the speaker/hearer *in vivo*.

As we have seen in the section on utterance and event classification, the distinction between classes of events is governed by categorical perception. Distinctions have to be embodied in a formal description of the communicative system when they are apparent to the actor, not when they correspond to some physical discontinuity in the stimulus array. We shall also see later that the relations between items which give a sequence of events its structural integrity are complex and not confined to adjacent items. These become much easier to detect when the judgements of the actor can be employed. On two counts, then, it seems more reasonable to start the investigation of behavioural sequences with an analysis of *judgemental data*—that is, with *emic methods* or the study of *competence*. It may be possible and fruitful later on to use *etic methods* to describe *performance*.

Social communication, like sentence construction, is creative. That is to say, we are not attempting to demarcate a finite set of possible communications, but rather to describe the common properties of an indeterminately large (and possibly infinite) set of well-formed symbol strings, which distinguish them from an equally large set of ill-formed strings. Furthermore, if this is to be part of a model of competence, the distinction between the two potentially infinite sets must be given a finite representation. This is facilitated by the use of recursive rules (1) or recursive rule combinations (2).

(1) $A \rightarrow A + B$

(2) $A \rightarrow B + C$
     $B \rightarrow A + D$

Just what is meant, then, by a rule of sequence? Let us suppose that in a corpus of dialogue between speakers A and B, recorded under conditions Z, we observe the regular occurrence of the sequence:

A: x
B: y

in which x denotes any member of the set of utterances having attribute X, or conforming to definition X, and similarly for y. Now let us postulate the existence of a rule of sequence which says that *x should be followed by y if Z obtains*. What does this imply about the use of these utterances which we could possibly test? Does it mean that

A: x
B: y

occurs, whereas

A: x
B: $\bar{y}$ (i.e. not y)

does not occur? This interpretation would produce an acute inductive problem, and for materials as variable as social interaction, would almost certainly be untrue. Does it mean that y is a more common sequitur to x than is $\bar{y}$? That is:

$$P(y \mid x) > P(\bar{y} \mid x)$$

If so, by how much must the probability be greater to be of any interest, and how may such probabilities effect the structure of larger strings? Does the rule mean that a sanction S is invoked if the rule is broken? So,

A: x
B: y
A: $\bar{S}$

and

A: x
B: $\bar{y}$
A: S

are observed, but

A: x
B: y
A: S

and

A: x
B: $\bar{y}$
A: $\bar{S}$

are never observed. Again we have an inductive problem.

We can defer the problem by saying that the rule *x should be followed by y* implies the rules *x followed by y should be followed by* $\bar{S}$ and *x followed by* $\bar{y}$ *should be followed by S*. That is all very well if we can set up S as belonging to a completely different level of behavioural analysis, which is not to be treated as units such as x and y. But it appears in the sequence of events in just the same way, and whatever governs the generation and propriety of x and y will exert the same influence upon S. Sanctions are not an independent yardstick, for the elicitation of social propriety. They are merely another piece in the social jig-saw and they raise the same doubts as all the others about their correct or incorrect use, and accurate or inaccurate identification.

Therefore if the rule *x should be followed by y* implies the rule *x followed by* $\bar{y}$ *should be followed by S* then this in turn implies that *x then* $\bar{y}$ *then* $\bar{S}$ *should be followed by S*, giving rise to sequences such as

    A: x
    B: ȳ
    A: S
    B: S̄

and

    A: x
    B: ȳ
    A: S̄
    B: S

Now there is real trouble: not only is the original inductive problem still present, but two others have been created.

1. There is now an infinite regressional series involved in the demonstration of any rule, since we could only infer that an utterance had been wrongly used from the occurrence of sanctions, if *those* sanctions were correctly used. That we deduce by looking for further sanctions which themselves may or may not be appropriate. This kind of regressional negotiation of propriety certainly can occur when someone feels he has been wrongly accused, but it is a poor criterion on which to base an entire discovery procedure.

2. The onus of responsibility for initiating sanctions can now fall upon the shoulders of the original miscreant, in that B could be required to reprimand A for not reprimanding B for his error in uttering ȳ!

Other attempts to infer rules from observed performance also run into similar difficulties. The interpretation that our rule implies that y *ought* to follow x would take us into the realms of ethics rather than psychology. If the rule is taken to imply that people believe y ought to follow x we still have to assign an arbitrary cut-off to the proportion of people who are to hold that belief for the rule to exist, and to find some account for those of different persuasion.

There are yet further problems. The likelihood of a sanction following some unspecified time after a breach of the rules does not enable us to identify the breach from the sanction, nor does it tell us what aspect of an item of behaviour is in conflict with the rules. If A sanctions B, for the things which B said last Tuesday afternoon, we still do not know whether the rules required B not to say those things; not to say them to A; not to say them on a Tuesday afternoon; not to say them *last* Tuesday afternoon, or whatever. Such difficulties may, however, be resolved by repeated observation.

Even if we overcome this complication and are able to deduce from the presence or absence of sanctions which rules have been kept or broken, we may end up with a few fragments of structure which cannot be synthesised into a unified theory. We may establish that j can follow i, and k can follow j, but we would still know nothing of the propriety or otherwise of the string ijk. In other words the influences which determine whether or not an utterance is used correctly in a given string, act configuratively rather than additively—a point which some traditional experimental techniques fail to recognise.

The main point thus far is that competence (linguistic or social) combines with many other influences to produce the totality of performance. Therefore competence is not uniquely specified by performance and *cannot be inferred from it*. This view is not universally accepted, and several workers in the field of sociolinguistics have set themselves the task of constructing 'grammars' which distinguish between the strings of utterances which are used and those which are not.

Let us put these abstract problems to do with the inference of rules from actions, or 'ought' from 'is', into a concrete setting. Consider the analogy with a game, and imagine the plight of a Martian observer at an Earth chess tournament observing that all games had (at least) two features in common: they all consisted of alternate moves by the two players, and they all started with the move, pawn to king four. The fact that the first is required by the rules and the second is a commonly preferred tactic is not immediately apparent to our Martian friend. Nor can he simply find the nearest chess player and ask 'What are the rules?', as the knowledge which makes rule following possible is often potential knowledge and not accessible to this kind of enquiry. One solution advocated by Garfinkel (1967) is to participate in the situation and 'breach' the structure by breaking the postulated rules. The use of sanctions would be taken to indicate that a rule had been broken. Our Martian friend, for example, would get a very different response for two such manoeuvres consisting of (i) making several moves per turn, and (ii) starting pawn to king's knight four. However this is a slow and sometimes alarming business and the results are by no means unequivocal. The disruption, use of remedial work and sanctions which are seen after a particularly bizarre act, may occur because a rule has been broken, or because the whole system of norms and expectations which reduce uncertainty in an interaction to a tolerable level has broken down. Thus the breacher identifies himself not simply as a breaker of rules, but also as a man of unpredictable and therefore potentially dangerous behaviour. Goffman (1971) makes the point very nicely, that the remedial work which may follow a breach is oriented less towards repairing the damage than to reaffirming that the offender does really know and believe in the rules and can be relied upon to follow them in future.

There is yet another way of eliciting rules which does not run into these difficulties, and that is to test specific hypotheses about rule-governed behaviour against the judgements of those who are familiar with and capable of using the rules. Our Martian could save a lot of time and trouble by asking one of the players whether the rules allow several moves per turn, and would arrive at an answer no less reliable and convincing than that produced by breaching. This method has obvious parallels with methods in social anthropology (Frake, 1964); with Chomsky's (1957) criteria of adequacy for linguistic rules; Harré and Secord's (1972) method of negotiating accounts, and current studies by Argyle et al. on judgements of social rule breaking. It seems the obvious approach to try first, as it is a method of discovering rules which is as common a part of everyday life as the rules themselves. In learning any new game it is the usual practice to consult someone who can already play, and ask 'Am I allowed to . . .?' rather than leaping on to the middle of the pitch to indulge in deliberately bizarre and unacceptable behaviour.

There is also the problem of generality. Studies of rule-governed behaviour seem all too often to address themselves to questions such as 'What are *the rules* of such and such a situation?', assuming that the rules are the rules and everyone has the same knowledge and opinion of them. It seems possible, however, that they are as much a matter of individual difference as of concordance, and to ask 'What are the rules?' is rather like asking 'What are *the preferences* for vegetables?' or 'What are *the memories* of last Friday afternoon?' Unless there is good evidence that a rule is ubiquitous within a given speech community or there is careful sampling of the population to whom the rule might apply, statements of the form 'It is a rule that . . .' are too vague and too unfalsifiable to be of much explanatory use.

Another problem has to do with the elicitation of 'local rules' and, more particularly, a special form of short term and restricted rule set up by contract. Breach of contract may manifest itself by disruption, sanction and remedy in much the same way as a breach of a more general rule, but there are dangers inherent in confusing the two. For example, if A says he will meet B under the clock at lunch time and does not turn up on time, our observation of sanctions would be very poor grounds for assuming that there is a rule requiring people to meet under the clock at lunch time, rather than that the rules require people who make an agreement to keep it. This form of behaviour which Austin called *commissive* (promises, undertakings, contracts, etc.) plays an important part in reducing uncertainty and facilitating interaction management. It is always a difficult cognitive task to predict the future behaviour of the people and things with which we interact. But individuals with memory, insight into their own future behaviour, and language, can allay the difficulties. They can agree with their coactors upon a mutually acceptable future, and bind themselves by the use of commissive acts to bring it about. Such acts could form part of the structure of plans, resolutions and commitments discussed by Miller, Galanter and Pribram (1960).

In the case of a unique 'made-to-measure' contract, such as 'I will meet you under the clock . . .', the existence of the deal is obvious, but other more standardised 'off-the-peg' contracts may go unnoticed or unrecognised by the outside observer. Thus an exchange such as

'Let's have a game of chess.'
'O.K.'

is a contract to behave in certain ways (specified by the rules of chess) and any departure from this is not only a breach of the rules of the game, but also of the social contract to play that game. These contracts are different from more general rules in several ways:

1. The operation of the contract may be deduced from actual behaviour prior to the episode in which the contracted behaviour is supposed to occur. In other words, a third party could observe the contract being made.

2. Sanctions need play no part in the identification of the contract.

3. Contracts can clearly only apply to voluntary behaviours, while general rules defined with respect to sanctions and disruptions alone might suggest that rules influence involuntary behaviour such as sudden illness, which would make a nonsense of the concept of rule. Using the judgements of the native social actor, however, the important distinction can be made between those voluntary behaviours upon which the rules may be said to act, and causally determined biological events.

The linguistic phenomenon of multiple articulation may have a counterpart in the structure of social behaviour. If so, the meaning of a particular unit could not be inferred with any ease from the meanings of its sub-components. In sentences it is common to find phonemes having no referential meaning making up morphemes which do have referents, and morphemes which have no propositional meaning making up sentences which embody propositions. In all probability we shall find in a similar way that with behaviour sequences and conversations, a whole string has a semantic representation which cannot be easily inferred from the semantic properties of its sub-components.

It may also be the case, as we have seen, that the syntactic properties of long strings are not related in any simple way to the properties of short ones. Let us suppose that a study of some kind of behavioural sequence has progressed (without insurmountable difficulty) to the stage where a number of event strings are available which are thought to be products of the system under study (that is, they are thought to be well-formed sentences, behaviour sequences with more than a specified probability of occurrence in given circumstances, or whatever), and which are thought to be correctly coded. The main problem then arises as to how one may set about detecting the sequential regularities in those strings. There are two major groups of techniques, the first consists of analytic methods, the second employs synthesis or simulation.

The starting-point of an analytic approach is usually a transitional frequency matrix or Markovian analysis. In its simplest form this shows the probability of a transition occurring between every possible pair of items (Raush, 1973). The chain of events so described may have a number of interesting properties. It may have a tendency to stick in a particular state (an *absorbing chain*) because there is a finite probability of the state being entered and an infinitesimal probability of its being left. Alternatively, a *cyclic chain* may form in which a succession of states tends to be repeated. The principal problem with a simple Markovian analysis is that it only relates each item of behaviour to one antecedent. It is true that some of the best studies of conversation structure to date have been confined to Markovian structures (e.g. Bales, 1953; Schegloff, 1968), but clearly a more sophisticated picture would be achieved by considering higher order sequences, where each item was related to several antecedents. This may also be achieved by a transitional frequency analysis, where transitions from a given string to a sequitur are described.

It is also possible to ascertain at what order of approximation the entropy of the sequence is minimised (Altman, 1965). It seems from such studies of various orders of statistical approximation to the sequence of English dialogue that about 3–5 previous utterances have to be considered in order to optimise prediction of each new utterance in the sequence (Pease & Arnold, 1973; Clarke, 1975). In addition to the various refinements that may be added to the procedures for describing the succession of events, there are a number of techniques for describing time intervals between successive occurrences of the same event, or adjacent occurrences of two different events. For example, the time between successive occurrences of a particular behaviour or class of behaviour may be plotted against the log of the frequency with which the interval is found. The resulting curve is a straight line of negative gradient for a behaviour which is randomly spaced in time, and shows a convexity towards the origin if the behaviour occurs in bouts, and a concavity towards the origin if the behaviour is 'over-spaced'. This technique is a modification of the ecological representation of survival data, and is therefore called the log-survivor function (Odum, 1971). A number of techniques for the ethological analysis of behaviour sequences may be found in Slater (1973). The problem with those techniques based on Markov analysis is that they require the chain to be *stationary*, that is the transitional probabilities must not change over time. Behaviour patterns, however, are usually non-stationary, and the likelihood of finding one behaviour after another may vary with a number of other variables concerning other behaviours in the sequence, situational and individual factors, and temporal and seasonal fluctuations.

It is in describing those sequences of events which show variable relations between adjacent items, while distant elements in the string may share an intimate structural relation, that synthetic techniques come to the fore. The current practice in generative linguistics, for example, is not to record a number of strings and analyse them, but to postulate a number of generative rules which will produce all and only the permissible strings in the language. This latter criterion is tested by using the judgements of the native speaker as mentioned earlier. The usual form of a generative rule is a rewriting operation

$$A \rightarrow B$$

in which one symbol or string is replaced by another. Clearly any generative operation replaces a pre-existing state of affairs with a subsequent one, so this notation can be used of all generative operations.

The basic generative processes must involve

addition
$$A \rightarrow A + B$$

deletion
$$A \rightarrow \phi$$

substitution
$$A \rightarrow B$$

and *transposition*
$$A + B \rightarrow B + A$$

The addition rule as it stands is ambiguous.

$$A \rightarrow A + B$$

could mean that the rule is to be used recursively, producing A, A + B, A + B + B, A + B + B + B . . ., which is the way such rules appear in Chomsky (1957), or as part of a Markov process in which A and B represent a succession of terminal elements, in which case any further rewriting must use rules beginning

$$B \rightarrow$$

or

$$A + B \rightarrow$$

To make this quite clear it is necessary to use an additional symbol, ' &', to represent the 'growth point' of strings which can only be rewritten at one locus. So, for example, the rule

$$A + \& \rightarrow A + B + \&$$

is quite unambiguous and cannot be used recursively. Indeed the symbol & need not have any 'meaning' at all to work in this way, provided it is used correctly.

We can now represent a variety of different rules and processes in the same form for comparison. A simple Markov chain would be generated thus:

$$A + \& \rightarrow A + B + \&$$
$$B + \& \rightarrow B + C + \& \text{ and so on.}$$

More commonly the rules would provide for a variety of different rewritings so one would see

$$A + \& \rightarrow A + B + \&$$
$$\rightarrow A + C + \&, \text{ and so on.}$$

Such a Markov process could be allowed to terminate at any point by the rules

$$\& \rightarrow \# \quad (\# \text{ is the symbol for a string delimiter})$$
$$\# \rightarrow \phi$$

or it could be made to terminate only after some suitable event D by the rule

$$D + \& \rightarrow D + \#$$
$$\# \rightarrow \phi$$

A higher order linear stochastic process producing a type 3 or finite state language (Chomsky, 1959) would use rules such as

$$A + B + \& \rightarrow A + B + C + \&$$

The more elaborate languages all use some kind of tree structure or nesting system. These can be generated by recursive

$$A \rightarrow A + B$$

or non-recursive rules

$$A \rightarrow B + C$$

Furthermore the rules can be context free

$$A \rightarrow B$$

or context dependent

$$P + A + Q \rightarrow P + B + Q$$
$$R + A + S \rightarrow R + C + S$$

Context free phrase structure rules characterise the type 2 language, and context dependent rules characterise the type 1 language (Chomsky, 1959).

Finally, in the type 0 language or transformational grammar a system of base rules, working by divergent substitution,

$$A \rightarrow B + C$$

produces a deep structure, which is transformed to surface structure by complex rules combining the operations of addition, deletion, substitution, and transposition:

$$A + B + C \rightarrow C + D + A$$

One could also imagine a grammar containing rules of convergent substitution

$$A + B \rightarrow C$$

Two other general classes of rule are worth considering here: rules which operate from left to right but allow for nesting

$$A + () + \& \rightarrow A + () + B + \&$$

and rules which work from left to right erecting non-terminal items from terminals. These are of particular interest to the student of interaction, because they allow one to produce nested structures without their having the paradoxical quality of being derived by two people from non-terminal antecedents which are never communicated. For example, if q and a are terminal items *question* and *answer* respectively, and X and Y are non-terminals of some kind, then the rules

$$q + \& \rightarrow q + X + \&$$
$$X + \& \rightarrow a + \&$$
$$\rightarrow Y + a + \&$$
$$Y \rightarrow q + a$$
$$\rightarrow q + Y + a$$

will generate a variety of permissible nested question answer sequences, but no cross-nested sequences. They will also assign the correct structural description to each string. Such rules may easily be used in computer simulations, where the machine has only to detect the presence of a left half rule in an incomplete character string, and replace it with the corresponding right half. Furthermore, the rules may be different for each actor or persona; may have probabilities attached to their use; and use different behaviour categories for different roles, if need be.

A string of the form AXB where B is present by virtue of A, and X is a sub-string of indeterminate length, is very hard to represent by a number of transitional frequencies between the *terminal elements* or observed outputs. It may, however, be described by transitional probabilities between *non-terminals* or a rule set of the following kind:

$$S \rightarrow A + X + B$$
$$X \rightarrow \ldots .$$

So far all these considerations have concerned the observed form of events or *surface structure*. The next consideration must be the semantic representation of behaviour sequences, and the possibility that this bears a closer resemblance to a *deep structure* than to the manifest surface structure.

Deep Structure

Some sequences of behavioural events are more likely to occur than others, and some are seen as well-formed while others appear to be ill formed. But that is not the whole story. The structural analysis of social behaviour should not just describe the tendency for certain successions of events to occur or to be preferred. It should also account for the way in which the observer draws different inferences about the actors from different behaviour sequences. Now it may well be the case that these inferences are a matter of simple correspondence between events and interpretations. For each observable string of events there is one and only one plausible interpretation, and for each conceivable state of psychological affairs (including such things as the attitudes, intentions and beliefs of the actors) there is only one possible behavioural manifestation. If that were so, then the matter of behavioural semantics would be very straightforward, and the semantic representation of a sequence of events could be related directly to the surface structure of the sequence. If, on the other hand, it turned out that there could be several interpretations of a single string of events (which did not simply correspond to the possible redescriptions of the surface structure itself), or that one state of psychological affairs for the actors could give rise to a number of behaviour sequences, then the correspondences between surface structure and semantic representation would be many-to-one and one-to-many. In such instances it may be useful to postulate a form of structural description which is a relative or transform of the surface structure, and which would be the behavioural counterpart of a linguistic deep structure.

Let us consider again the analogy between social interaction and chess. Many interesting parallels exist whichever kind of chess is envisaged, but the comparison becomes particularly apt when one considers the form of chess which enthusiasts play by letter or telephone. The game consists of an exchange of messages, as far as the outside observer is concerned. He could intercept these messages and try to find a sequential pattern among them, which is effectively what the discourse analyst does when trying to interrelate successive utterances. But to understand the game of chess, the observer would have to appreciate that the messages were not just an abstract text, governed only by their own interrelations, but rather the product of the players' world views (the private board which each keeps up to date as the game progresses, his *deep structure* for the game), and the rules for the modification and elaboration of particular states of play. These are like the generative rules of a language, particularly the base rules. Of course there are other factors as well, such as the strategic concerns of the players, but they are characteristics of particular games rather than 'the game of chess' in all its possible forms, so they do not concern us for the time being.

It might seem that this mysterious hidden structure could be attributed to almost any system, but in fact a communication system may relate semantics to transmitted forms in a number of ways, not all of which employ deep structures. In a very simple kind of code, which one might call a *unit code*, there would be one symbol for each message. In some respects marine flag codes are like this. One flag conveys one message and two flags convey two messages. This makes for a very limited signalling repertoire, which can only be expanded by the use of more symbols, or by using the symbols in combination. In a *sequence code* there is a different meaning for each succession of symbols. Such a code may have a syntax, in which case only certain kinds of sequence are permissible and meaningful; or it may have no syntax, in which case any symbol combination is meaningful, and the only rules of interest are those relating different sequences to their different meanings. An example of such a code is the system of Arabic numerals (omitting for the sake of this example any operators or symbols other than the integers 0 to 9). Different integer combinations represent different quantities, but all integer combinations represent *some* quantity. In a more elaborate code still, the same sequence of events may represent different meanings depending on the grouping of items and their interrelations. So a sentence like 'They were eating apples' is ambiguous because of the uncertain relations of *eating* in *were—eating* or *eating—apples*. Such a code might be called a *group code*. Finally, there are the *elliptical* or *enigmatic codes* which even a description of intersymbol relations cannot disambiguate, and these are the codes which might be said to have a distinct *deep structure*. It seems likely that any succession of social behaviours will fall into the latter category, and require the postulation of some kind of deep structure.

The role of the deep structure in the generation of social behaviour is open to different interpretations. Perhaps the safest thing to say for the time being is that it bears a global resemblance to the actor's cognitive structures as do the generative rules, in so far as they embody the same information. That does not necessarily mean, though, that they have a feature-by-feature or operation-by-operation correspondence to the generative process in the real social actor. The real operations by which the actor arrives at particular performances can only be studied in detail when we have a better conception of the behaviour patterns which result. Then we may be able to tell whether the rules or hypothetical operations which produce all and only the acceptable behaviour sequences in an abstract 'behaviour grammar' do describe the generative processes of the social actor *in vivo*.

In conclusion, human social behaviour has an all important temporal structure, which is similar in many respects to that of a language. Analytic operations performed on the behaviour stream by the native actor, in the light of a number of semantic considerations which cannot be inferred from behavioural observation alone, should yield structural regularities akin to a grammar. To arrive at this point, one would first have to segment the behaviour stream to produce a succession of discrete events, then classify the events and study the relations which may obtain between them in orderly behaviour sequences. The classification of events (or paradigmatic structure) and the sequential patterns formed by event classes (or syntagmatic structure) are inextricably related. The semantic representation of the behaviour stream may suggest the presence of an independent deep structure of behaviour.

The Rise of the Rule: Mode or Node?

PETER ROBINSON

The title is chosen because the psychology of social behaviour seems to me to be marked by more fashion than is necessary (hence Mode) and less growth than is desirable (hence Node). We are too ready to abandon what has already been achieved. Instead of carefully and studiously inspecting our past, and sifting it in the light of our new enthusiasms, we dispense with it and leap on to some band-wagon. By doing this we manage to avoid a lot of hard work; it saves us reading what has gone before. We can move to instant fame and then strut and fret our hour upon the stage.

I am reminded of this disposition by an examination question set recently about the new five-volume Lindzey and Aronson *Handbook of Social Psychology*. If you are fortunate enough to have seen this giant, and if you found that you were strong enough to lift and open it, you may have discovered that it contains a substantial quantity of social psychology. The examination question was, 'Is Lindzey and Aronson a tombstone or a milestone?' These were the alternatives offered. It could of course be seen as a millstone. But why not a foundation stone of some sort? Why do we have to consider throwing knowledge away? Why are we tempted to see the demise of great masters as an achievement? I have an associated suspicion that those examinees who argued for the tombstone verdict may have found it easier to obtain high marks than those who said it was a milestone. But how many examinees (or examiners) would have studied all five volumes sufficiently conscientiously to pass informed and humble judgement? Interestingly enough, this disposal habit is not characteristic of the intellectual development of children. As they grow, children reinterpret and reorganise their data and their ways of thinking. I am wondering whether we should not be a little more child-like. Perhaps we should persevere a little longer with the study of our past and try to reorganise it in the light of the new ideas that we have and the new thinking we achieve.

If you wish to be learned rather than child-like, you may prefer to cite Popper's (1968) recommendation that science needs to be both conservative and revolutionary. We seem to have misinterpreted Popper's suggestion that a good theory is one that is easily refuted. What was meant was that the basis for disconfirmation of predictions should be clear. It was not intended that we should believe that easily refuted hypotheses were good, willy nilly. We do seem to have been prone to assert the consequent and then to rush on, mistaking cleverness for wisdom.

If one looks through the social psychology of the last fifteen to twenty years, one finds that topics and approaches have been born, have grown, and have died, occasionally to be resurrected. Topics such as attitude structure and change, small group behaviour, sociometry, social facilitation (there is a slight resurrection in that one); approaches such as Information theory, Games theory, Hullian theory, Psychoanalytic theory, and the attempts to articulate these. How much consideration is given to these in current undergraduate courses? If you look in the *Psychological Abstracts* at the number of entries under such headings, you can plot the rise and fall of each graph; a trickle accumulates into an ascent that attenuates to a plateau, and then down comes the line until finally there is but a dribble of people persevering with that topic or framework.

What is *à la mode* at the moment? We seem to have taken a recent unrisky decision to rid ourselves of risky shift, but verbal and non-verbal communication have risen and remain pre-eminent. So far, we have seen at least two main approaches to problems in these areas: there is the 'Let's treat these activities as skills' preference, and the more recent 'Let's treat them as rule-governed behaviour' perspective. It is the rule-governed behaviour that we are going to talk about here. This approach appears to have its cognitive origins in philosophy (moral and otherwise), linguistics and ethnomethodology, but it seems to have arisen affectively out of an exasperation with the ritual nature of much of the experimentation in social psychology. People have become irritated at the sight of more and more trivial little two-page

articles reporting minor methodological variations on minor variations of a perhaps long-forgotten theme. Form without substance may
have been an ideal for Plato, but it is decadent nonsense for any species
of empirical scientist.

What about this new approach of rule-hunting? It is full of vigour.
It makes many valid criticisms, both of the technology and of the
methodology of much social psychology. What I am hoping is that it
will not shortly suffer the same fate as the topics and approaches I have
mentioned. I hope its rise will not be followed by a rapid decline. I will
not object if it wanes for the right reasons, but I would not like to see it
disappear for the wrong ones. So in this paper I would like to draw
attention, if I can, to one or two warning signs, signs which, if they are
not heeded, may be succeeded by a decline of interest. I also intend to
make some suggestions for development.

As a small example of one kind of danger, we can consider the
attacks on Popper and the Mechanised Model of Man in Harré and
Secord's book, *The Explanation of Social Behaviour* (1972). Some of us
might be tempted to say that the case against both Popper and the
model is overstated. Approaches can find themselves in trouble because
they misrepresent earlier approaches. There are central features and
peripheral features to any approach. 'Are the criticisms of Popper really
valid?' is a question about a peripheral feature only, but such a query
might set off an inquiry that showed that one or two or those criticisms
were invalid. It might then be suggested that the whole approach must
be unsound because it is founded on slightly unsound criticisms of
Popper. The logic may not be impeccable, but not all human thinking
is either. Slightly dirty bath-water may emerge as a reason for disposing
of the baby. Although, if the baby is inwardly healthy, such tempta-
tions may be more readily resisted, it is better to avoid such skirmishes.
If we turn to more important matters, I would summarise my present
concern in the expression of a wish that the Harré and Secord approach
now seek to define its limitations and draw its boundaries. I will raise
a number of points related to this general issue. The four main ones are
not independent of each other and they are not all original. Some are
made in the book itself, but perhaps I can give them greater salience for
subsequent discussion. What then are the four points?

1. I think the time is coming when we shall need to have tighter
definition of some of the key terms. I think this is both desirable and
necessary. It is appropriate at some early phase in new ventures to say

'I do not know what I mean by these words, but I have some vague ideas, and it may be worth sticking with them; hopefully some clearer definitions will emerge'. Such a hope must eventually be realised. As with all everyday words, the term 'rule' is one of those polymorphous items with messy edges. Which senses of it are to be refined and converted into one or more technical terms for talking about social behaviour?

2. Where some specification of rules is a necessary part of a critical description of phenomena, and perhaps constitutes an explanation as well, is this specification also a sufficient basis for maintaining that the phenomena have been totally explained? That is (and we shall look at some instances of this later), if we find out the rules of the game, whatever the particular game is, will this suffice? Is an exposure of the rules a necessary discovery we have to make on our way to a more complete story? I will suggest that for some topics it may be enough, but that for others it will not be.

3. Related to this second point is the question of when is rule-hunting not a sensible exercise? I think we ought to try to be explicit about the topics in social psychology for which the hunting of rules is not likely to be an appropriate pursuit. In which fields should we not bother to look for rules at all? I can think immediately of problems in the study of attitudes, categorisation, motivation, and problem-solving activities of various sorts, where a rule model does not appear to have application. If we can say where rule models are not appropriate and can see why they are not, this may help us to say why they are useful where they are appropriate. This point will be handled only in passing, but it surely merits extended consideration by someone soon.

4. Where it is appropriate to chase the rules, I would like to argue two points:
(i) We have problems of precision. We must try not to push solutions of problems too far. Some rules may be very messy, while others may be precise and clear. We need to be clear about which are which. We should not try to push for precision beyond what is warranted by the way things actually work.
(ii) People's relationships to rules can differ. Their beliefs about the nature, the durability, the legitimacy, the perceived necessity, and the origin of rules can differ. Their understanding and knowledge of the

rules that are supposed to govern their behaviour may also differ. How important is this, both for the way we go about looking at behaviour and for our attempts at explaining what people are doing? The accounts that people give of their behaviour are not always useful. It may be indecent for them to tell you either why they do what they do or even what the rules are. It may be imprudent or unwise for them to mention them or to make them explicit. They may be just incapable of doing so. I am a bit worried that what is true of Hampstead man, the sort of well-educated Englishman who reads the *Guardian* and enjoys Scarlatti, is not true of lions, children, small and simple isolated cultures in Papua New Guinea, or perhaps even rather large subcultural groups in any complex caste or class-based society. That is what I shall try to argue later, but only with reference to children.

The Use of 'Rule'

Let us look briefly at definitions of 'rule'. Fortunately, Harré and Secord differ from many other recent users of 'rule' in that they do provide us with a definition: 'In order to achieve A (the act), do $a_1 \ldots a_n$ (the actions) when S (the occasion or situation) occurs.' This is a general form of a rule (they say more about the problem of course, but this is one format of a rule). One might ask how this corresponds to the uses of philosophers, other social psychologists, linguists, game players, headmasters, bureaucrats and law drafters? Does this correspond to their use of the word 'rule'?

If we look at some examples, I am afraid that we find a considerable diversity of uses. Linguists' rules do not appear to fit the above definition; their rewrite rules, their phrase-structure rules and their transformational rules are not presented in that form. They are long sequences of symbols which convert basal ideas into grammatical realisations that ordinary people can read and understand. Covertly they may be similar, but overtly they are not. Developmental psychologists talk about children acting as though rules were governing their behaviour. If when a ball of plasticine is rolled into a sausage the child reports an increase in amount, it may be claimed that he is using the rule, 'If it's longer than before, then there is more of it'. Buses have 'No Smoking' signs in them. Games have statements like, 'There should be eleven players in each team'; or perhaps, more appropriate here, 'If a player fails to run his hoop or hit another ball, his turn ends'. 'There is to be no running along school corridors.' I will not read out anything from a Government form specifying any sort of rule—we have not got time to hear the details of the conditions under which peanuts do and do not attract Value Added Tax, and few of us would understand them anyway. Let us note that none of these have Harré and Secord's 'In order to achieve A . . .' explicitly at the front of them. Such a preface may be implicit and we shall need to sort out when it is, and when it is not.

Three points may be noted about technical and ordinary uses of the word 'rule': (i) we have a *diversity* of linguistic forms for expressing what people generally consider to be rules, (ii) people also use other labels in identical or related ways, *viz.* words like 'regulation', 'norm', 'order', and 'law', and (iii) within the social sciences themselves there appears to be a further spreading out of ordinary usage. I do not think, even if you pick your man from Hampstead Heath rather than from the Clapham omnibus, you will find that he will use 'rule' in the same way as the developmental psychologists or the linguists use the word. With a diversity of forms, a diversity perhaps of concepts as well, we can begin to see some of the difficulties.

It does not seem to me that what has happened is unusual. We often cull a word from ordinary usage in order to convey new ideas to our colleagues. To take a word from everyday life and to begin to use it in a technical sense is quite acceptable, but we have to be clear when and how we are doing this and when we are making recommendations about the way ordinary usage could be improved. Let us hope that we eventually manage to be precise and clear in what we mean by this term. I think the complications have arisen partly because we are short of separate single words to refer to a variety of meanings. Everyday language does not have the lexical variety to distinguish between these different sorts of 'rules'—if they are different. If we just look briefly at some of the aspects of the definitional problem, we may be able to say something constructive about the way forward.

There are various oppositions that can help to define and locate 'rule'. The dictionary and ordinary use require a rule to be general in application and not to be unique to place, time, and persons. A sense of obligation and not just of habit is intended. Perfect regularity of behaviour is not required: people do not always have to follow the rule for it to be said that their behaviour is rule-governed. Perhaps we will want to include some notion of awareness on the part of the person following or not following a rule. Although this is not required with the transformational rules of the linguists, do we, in social psychology, want to include some notion of awareness on the part of the person following or not following a rule. If so, an awareness of what? Perhaps the awareness might be limited to the breach of rules? Less often mentioned are the consequences of not following rules which may have to be brought into any definition. We label specific acts of rule-breaking in games in different ways. For some events we refer to 'cheating' and for others 'ceasing to play the game'. We may have sanctions like the penalties imposed on some player. In social life, there may be fines or punishment for infractions. People also run the risk of being mis-understood if they are acting on different rules from others. Perhaps this is a sanction, perhaps not. An examination of the various ways in which we talk about failing to observe or breaking rules might facili-tate the elaboration of distinctions between different types of rule. Finally, and this is a direct extract from Harré and Secord, invoking a rule provides some sort of reason for the particular behaviour men-tioned. Part, at least, of the 'why', 'what' and 'when' of a particular act can be answered by an appeal to a rule.

These then are some of the problems. It seems to me that these matters have to be analysed thoroughly, and that the analyses need to be followed by syntheses. What is giving an account as a rule? How many senses do we wish the term to have and which of these aspects of the concept are finally to be included in it? At least we can begin to be clearer about the focus of our enquiries. Although there has already been some conceptual wood clearing, there now needs to be some more ruthless dissection. Additionally, I think we now have to move towards some kind of policy of afforestation. We need to start making stricter recommendations as to how this word and its associates are to be used.

Rules in Descriptions and Explanations of Social Behaviour

Where are we to use 'rules' in our enquiries once it is agreed that they are appropriate constituents of a particular analysis? In any field of enquiry we need first to formulate our problem, then we have to carry out investigations, then we have to process the data, and finally we have to interpret and communicate our results, if any. However, our methodology and technology changes as we get to know more about whatever it is we are investigating. At the beginning of any enterprise we are apt to rely upon intuitive concepts based on, or derived from, ordinary language. We invoke these in the first place because we have observed something odd or because something in our environment does not quite make sense. Perhaps we read something strange in a novel, or notice an oddity in a play, and we judge there to be a problem in the area. We are jogged into an awareness of something problematic, and we begin to think about it. We make a few guesses as to what might be going on. We make a few enquiries with a variety of loose procedures. We observe cases in detail. We ask subjects for reports. We rely on people who seem to be experienced in this oddity in some way. We allow people to use their own response categories when they talk to us about these matters. We look, listen, guess and interpret. This is the beginning, or should be, of any enterprise. We can contrast this initial fumbling with the endgame. By that time we have highly refined multivariate experiments, with all independent and dependent variables measured as precisely as their conceptual status allows, experiments in which we see whether or not the deduced new prediction from a tight theory is quantitatively falsified. To achieve this state is the objective of the game, for some people, for some problems. Do Harré and Secord say that is where they would like to go, or do they think we ought not to be trying to go there? Is it the case that rules are something we have to find out about on the way to this end-point or will they be sufficient in themselves? What I wish to illustrate is that for some problems it might be appropriate to end with rules, but that for others it would not.

I have already asked whether one of the reasons that Harré and Secord are so upset about contemporary social psychology is that they see its practitioners rushing in at the wrong end of the enterprise. And it is true that we are prone to rush in at the final stages and pretend to be measuring everything. Sociologists call this 'ritualising the means'. Undergraduates are often presented with the endgame as an idea. There is the ideal. Now aspire to it and apply it. We do not train people to observe. We do not train them to play about with ideas; we do not even give them the opportunity to play with ideas. We are wont to offer neat little discriminations, often methodological minutiae, and the acolyte psychologists are headed towards their two page articles, with correct design, correct statistics, and a conclusion that more research is to be done in order to qualify just where the experimental manipulation is having an effect on this particular variable, if it is. By this stage, in reality, nobody could care less about the issues any more. I want to know whether it is an indignation against the dangers of misapplying this ideal which is important to Harré and Secord, or whether there is more to it than that. I think we need to separate those cases where the pursuit of the 'ideal' is inappropriate in terms of contemporary knowledge and understanding from those cases where it is inappropriate because of the nature of the problems themselves.

What are they asking for in terms of rules? One goal is to identify significant acts in social behaviour. Let us look and find out what is meant by 'an act'. Let us not invent a pantheon of logically possible variables, but let us identify which acts actually have significance. Let us categorise episodes. And to this end, we can use case studies, reports by people, and naturalistic observation to find out about these matters. This begins to look very much like my caricature of the beginning of any scientific enterprise. To begin at the beginning is sensible, but whither thence?

May I just look at two problems in the heartland of social behaviour to see how we might run with rules and to see whether there is a need to go beyond them. The first problem concerns forms of address, the selection of Title, Title Last Name, Last Name, First Name, or Multiple Names (i.e. a variety of words) as means of addressing or referring to others. What do we call other people in our society? This has also been examined with the personal pronouns in languages which have different pronouns for 'you' (Brown and Gilman, 1960), and with a variety of other forms in other languages in other societies (Ervin-Tripp, 1969). We can identify the significant lexical units of the language clearly and unambiguously. Life is not quite as simple, however, because, to have their normal significance, these and other units and structures have to be uttered properly and sincerely with all the other variables in the context set at appropriate values. It is not enough just to say 'Sir' and hope that it will not matter how you say it. But how do we choose which address form to use? Do we say, 'Professor', 'Prof. Smith', 'Smith', 'Roy' or 'Diddums'?

Susan Ervin-Tripp has set out her rules of selection as a succession of binary choices posed as closed questions. Is the person an adult or not? Is the setting status marked or not? Is the name known? She produces a flow chart whose detailed character need not detain us, but whose final feature is a series of arrow points on the right-hand side which link up to Title, Last Name, Mr. + Last Name, Mrs. + Last Name, Miss + Last Name, Title, First Name, Multiple Name and ? (which means we do not know what to call the other person). There is her list. These are the facts. The flow chart gives the facts but no interpretation. She calls these rules sociolinguistic rules of alternation. If we know she calls somebody Mrs. + Last Name, then we can work out from her diagram whether they are married, older, etc. If we know their attributes, we can work out the address form. We find out which statuses she treats as significant choice points, and we can mark out her status categories. The diagram fits one of Harré and Secord's requirements, namely that it constitutes some sort of explanation of particular events: with the diagram we can now cite a *particular* case as an instance of her more general rules. But surely this is not the end? We need to go further. For an explanation of why she calls these people by these names, and why she uses these particular status categories, we need to go further , and in doing so we will possibly rely on something like Brown's template (1965).

Brown's power semantic and solidary semantic give a simple general framework of two abstract aspects underlying any relationship between people. Brown states that forms of address are used to indicate differential power or similarity of power between two participants and what he calls solidariness. This is an unfortunate choice of terminology. It is used to refer to interdependence of some kind. This may be based on intimacy or familiarity. It may be an interdependence deriving from a joint need to achieve some external goal as on an Arctic expedition. It could be based on family ties or *esprit de corps*. If people move towards greater solidariness, the forms of address change, but reciprocity and symmetry will characterise the use at each stage of the relationship. On the power semantic, inequality between the participants is often marked by non-reciprocal, that is asymmetrical, forms of address. You call me 'Mr.'; I call you 'Jill'. Without a guide book containing rules of interpretation, we cannot immediately guess from this example which way round matters are, but we can account for variation in the lexical terms used for forms of address against this template. The template is a common one in social psychology, in which many problems are associated with power and solidariness. If we explain the differential use of terms in this manner, then we are able to say why Susan Ervin-Tripp uses the terms she does.

I think Harré and Secord can say, 'Fine, these propositions are rules'. In our society, in order to show superior power, what I have to do is insist upon defining the terms of address and make them asymmetric. In this context I would have to get you to use my title, but I would use as familiar and as friendly a term for you as possible. This can still be a rule, but note we have already used 'rule' twice here, once without the 'in order to', and now the Harré and Secord variant with a preposed 'in order to'. Is this the end of the problem if we can fit our data on to this?

We can proceed to ask why these rules and not others can be used to achieve these ends, and if you read Brown you will find that his story about pronoun use moves into an historical, sociological story stretching back to the Roman Empire and its two emperors. The problem ceases to be of immediate interest to social psychology. Where the 'you', 'thou' and 'thee' came from and went to is fascinating history, but not social science. Why the Javanese have eighty-five different terms of address for other Javanese, and a whole special lexis and verbal system devoted to address as well, is a comparative sociological problem and not one of immediate interest to social psychology. Why any conflict in choice is resolved in favour of power over solidariness or the other way round is again likely to be a socio-logical problem. It may well be, I think, that where there is a clearly defined categorical set of possibilities, like forms of address, Brown's story marks an end point for social psychology. We do not really need to know any more.

It is eventually up to us to decide. I think we may be a little premature to close matters this early, since we have not actually collected much data in the field. We may find that there are various systematic irregu-larities, when we look to see what people actually call other people. In our society, particularly, the matters may be somewhat messy and full of interesting problems. Perhaps a continued pursuit would still be for rules. We could still be chasing rules, but might be asking about the meaning of particular ways of breaking rules. These would themselves be rules, and we could still incorporate our stories within a rule model.

I think, however, that we could proceed to yet further problems. When we found diversity in the messiness which we would undoubtedly encounter, we would probably need to concern ourselves with who cares about these rules and why. What sort of people worry about getting the forms of address right and what sort of people do not? Who is good at using these devices for regulating relationships and who is not? Or we could approach from other starting-points. What about authoritarians? Would we expect that high authoritarians are going to have very clear rules about etiquette? Would they like to be able to buy a book so that they would know exactly what to call everybody else and have no problems of ambiguity or any of those other sources of distress from which they suffer? Or perhaps we can compare extroverts and introverts? An image emerges of introverts hiding away, desperately trying not to call anybody anything, and of extroverts backslapping themselves into multiple-naming on first encounters. If we were to ask about these individual or group differences, the questions would not be concerned with discovering or constructing rules. They would be about variations among people in their knowledge, interest, enthusiasm and concern about the rules. There are more questions than the simple 'What are the rules of the game?' But the rules must be discovered before the other questions can be asked (see Robinson, 1972).

My second example may be more serious. Distance between people can signify something about the social relationship between them. I believe the story has been told around Oxford that eye contact is also relevant to what goes on between people. So are forms of address. What are the differences between forms of address on the one hand and distance and eye contact on the other? Are there differences? All three are used for signalling power and friendship, for playing solidary and power games, but they are different as well, are they not? For example, distance and eye contact have functions other than those of sending messages. Distance maintenance avoids suffering unpleasant odours. Eye contact is allegedly used for facilitating the smooth switching from speaker to listener role. Eye contact is used to regulate social interaction and for seeking information as well as for playing the power/friendship game. These are other functions, one of them used deliberately, two of them unlikely to be so deliberate in use.

Not only are there other functions, there are other determinants of choice. There are contextual factors which force changes in the available range of values. If you are caught in a lift with another person, this is different from being in a room or in an open field. The situation will affect what gap you leave between yourself and somebody else. The relative heights, deafness, blindness or short-sightedness of the participants will influence the choices. There was a beautiful instance of this in Oxford. Michael Argyle gave a demonstration at a British Psychological Society Conference to show that tall people and short people talking to each other would stand at a greater distance apart than people of equal height. The members of the audience duly waited to be amazed by this demonstration. The little fellow came in and walked right up to the tall man, leaving only an absurdly minimal space between them. Inevitably, when he went over to sit down in his seat, he reached to his friend, who handed him back a pair of glasses. Michael did not see this exchange and could not work out why everybody was laughing. Although the distance maintained between people is supposed to have meaning in terms of the friendship in a relationship, other factors are also relevant. There are different determinants and different functions.

We can also note that both the range and type of variation is different. Distance is continuously variable and amenable to speedy change. It is not like 'Mr.' versus 'Mrs.' or 'tu' versus 'vous', where a categorical distinction is made. With eye contact the amount of time spent in mutual gaze is continuously variable. Do these continuously variable features have characteristics that the categorical ones do not? They may have. They afford ambiguity and allow an indefiniteness of meaning that preclude capture in a book of etiquette.

The Precision of Rules

This leads into the first aspect of the fourth point about the pursuit of precision in those areas where rule-hunting is an appropriate sport. We must avoid attempts at over-precision in the formulation of rules. As I have suggested, not only may the operative variables be continuous and not discrete, but in any particular situation we have to think of variables acting in combination. We have combinations of values of variables which do not give unambiguous answers. If we use the list of posture, distance, gesture, eye contact and the other features that Michael Argyle (1969) spells out, what happens when these give discordant information? Argyle has demonstrated that where people are signalling superiority in some ways and inferiority in others, the perceiver does not come to an unequivocal judgement. Similarly with the friendly–unfriendly dimension. People do make judgements, but they are clearly aware that not all values of variables are giving a consistent answer; they mention confusion and confusedness and lack of confidence (cf. Argyle et al., 1970). One of the problems is that there are many variables that enter into any judgement you have to make, but in the end you make just one judgement, unless of course you are able and willing to defer your decision. You have to decide whether your protagonist is friendly or not, confused or hypocritical, or whatever else it is that you need as a basis for your action in the situation. I think this difficulty arises partly because most people are not conscious of the rules of the game, partly because people are trying to deceive other people (they are trying to pass themselves off as something they are not), and partly because relationships are not static.

I suspect that ambiguity in cues makes it easier for relationships to change smoothly. There can be an overt and formal attempt to change. 'May I stop calling you Miss Smith? May I call you Jill?' In my youth one could have used a formal request to change the form of address. However, one could also take advantage of these continuously variable cues. You take Miss Smith's hand to help her cross the road. Now, do you leave it there a bit too long when you reach the other side and how does she react to this? When you are dancing, and your hands move to exert a little extra pressure does she respond to this? If she says 'You're being too familiar', you can say, embarrassedly, 'I'm sorry, my hand just sort of moved' or truculently, 'I was only saving you from being trodden upon' or weakly, 'I did not notice'. Perhaps these examples suggest a certain personal ineptness at the game, but they illustrate the point. We have various ways of saving face in such situations, and ambiguity enables a quick test–operate–test–exit exchange in which both participants can arrive at a face-saving solution to any change proposed by one but rejected by the other participant. If this is so, it means that we cannot have precision in the values of the variables that we are going to use for achieving change because there has to be some ambiguity in order to achieve the change in the first place. Categorical signals are useful for static relationships, but ambiguous signals are useful for facilitating change. We will need to cope with this problem eventually.

The Relationship between People and Rules

The final worry about situations where rule-hunting is appropriate was that we need to appreciate that people's relationships to rules can differ. This may be illustrated in developmental social psychology. Let us briefly consider marbles, children and Piaget. Contrary to occasionally heard criticisms, Piaget (1932) did work with more than three children and he did sometimes work with non-middle-class children from the back streets of Geneva, and marbles is a case in point. He looked at the ways in which children of different ages played marbles. He played the Garfinkel game, and appropriately he was a bit dim. He did not quite understand how the game was played; sometimes he deliberately broke the rules to see how the children would react. He eventually came out with a story about the development of children's thinking about rules and their behaviour in relation to those rules. His story is in fact more complicated than it is usually represented in secondary sources, but I can quickly run through a travesty of the truth.

What does the child between the ages of two and four do if you give it some marbles? It eats them or plays eggs and nests with them. If you repeat the procedure and give it marbles on subsequent occasions, Piaget says you will find that the child engages in crystallised rituals, repetitive actions. When the child is given the marbles, you cannot be sure which of his particular rituals he will go through, but he will eventually move into one of them and then he will run off a sequence of actions, treating the marbles as eggs in a nest of whatever it is that his game in fact involves. If you ask him about his actions, there is no understanding of 'rules': he does not know what you are talking about. Piaget says—and he calls these 'motor rules' of behaviour—that although these actions are not rule-governed, they are nevertheless necessary as a basis for subsequent development.

It is out of frustration of the rituals when the child is interfered with by older children and adults in certain situations that he experiences conflict (or Bruner's word 'trouble'). The eventual solution of the conflict will be in terms of coming to play a slightly different game of marbles. This leads to the second main stage which involves what Piaget called the morality of constraint: the heteronomous stage— being subject to the law of somebody else. In this, the child will first of all imitate the actions of other people. He will play by himself with no intention of winning, but eventually this gives way to trying to win and a concern about the rules. If you actually look at what he is doing, however, he is very frequently breaking the rules which he says are governing his behaviour. There is very little relationship between the rules that the child appears to be playing by and the ones he says he is using. If you ask him about these rules, he says they are obligatory and unchangeable. They are authenticated by parents. If you read Piaget, at least one little boy was quite happy to say his father was older than God and it was his father that thought up the rules and not God. At the same time there is the notion of rules being eternal, unchangeable, and obligatory. He has to obey these rules, and yet at the same time he is breaking them at every turn. This is Piaget's morality of constraint.

Round about seven or eight the child experiences further conflicts. From the diversity of games encountered, which he meets in playing with other, often older, children he comes to learn that there are different rules. There will be a clash between his own beliefs and those of the other children which eventually leads to a resolution in what Piaget calls the rational, autonomous morality of cooperation. By now the child's behaviour corresponds to the rules and he will tell you that the rules he is playing by are arrived at by mutual consent among the players. They are arbitrary and can be changed. You can invent new rules if other people will agree to them, but these must involve skill and effort on the part of the winner. You cannot just invent silly rules, they must be in accordance with the spirit of the game. Where did they come from? Children invented them, and they are handed down. By this stage there is behaviour which corresponds to the rules, which are seen as contingent and established by mutual consent. This is a travesty of Piaget's account, but we can note some points about it.

The child begins with the motor rules of ritual. He then proceeds to claim that they are unchangeable, obligatory and authenticated by parents or some other authority figure, but flouts them. He emerges finally into the self-imposed rational autonomous stage. I would like to make three points in this connection:

1. There are developmental changes in the awareness of rules. Furthermore, the nature of the rules to which he subscribes changes both in terms of their content and their authority. These changes are alleged to be provoked by conflict and its resolution. There is in fact little evidence for this, but the main point would be the theoretical one that conflict can lead to change. If it is so with children, is it not the same with us? Do we need to see alternatives before we can become aware of the meaning of what we do? Do people realise the validity of what we have said about the features of interaction until they see other people doing something different or find that mistakes of interpretation are being made? This would be the first point: the perception of difference leads to conflict, and conflict leads to changes in awareness of the nature of rules, both in terms of content and authority.

2. May I fly a kite and suggest that the rules become more sensible as children get older, both in terms of what the rules contain and in terms of their relationship to the kind of authority cited to underpin

them? I am prepared to try to argue that they are more sensible, that they are more rational, and that they are more adaptive. I would suggest that marbles is not a special case. We could perhaps extend the generalisations not only to greetings and forms of address, but to social interaction generally and perhaps to the distribution of wealth in society as well. Perhaps mankind is moving towards some more rational morality. You can have rules which are more sensible and less sensible. As society develops, we might expect a similar shift, both at the level of individuals and at the level of social institutions and organisations.

3. Various combinations of the relationship between 'action' and 'report' are revealed. Harré and Secord say that it is reasonable to start by asking people about the rules they follow. I agree. Start by asking people. But what possibilities are there? Well, there are three in the Piagetian analysis. First of all you can have regular action, but no report of the rule. Then you can have irregular action and a clear report of rules, or you can have regular but varied action, and a clear corresponding report of the rules. Presumably more than three forms of relationship are possible. As I have already suggested, people may be unable or unwilling to accept that there are rules governing their behaviour. They may be relative hedonists who just will not accept the verbal formulation of any rules; this is supposed to be the case for a minority of university undergraduates, according to Kohlberg and Kramer (1969). There is also deliberate flouting of both verbal and non-verbal rules. Bloomsbury man will deliberately flout the rules of conventional society. We have an unwillingness to reveal the rules. I cannot say anything systematic about this but one suspects that Dockland man, the industrial man, behaves like this. There are rules governing what happens on the shop floor, but you will never be told what these are. You have to find out for yourself. This can be a way of keeping strangers out of the group, but of course high status people in our society will employ similar devices. You have got to know how to join the club. Its members may not necessarily want you to join their club. It would be dreadful if you managed to sneak in with one of your extra good royal performances, and they would discover too late that you should not be there. So I suspect that there are situations in which there are difficulties in finding out what the rules are. Sometimes knowledge is power and sometimes this knowledge is of rules.

The possible and actual relationships between 'reports' and 'rules' and the occasions of differential relationships will need to be spelled out and then investigated. Harré and Secord allow for a diversity of relationships, but I am frightened that unless these issues are given detailed consideration their complexity will be distorted and reduced to a generalisation that people can report the rules to which they voluntarily subscribe. We know from studies of serial reproduction how people distort and simplify what they read (Bartlett, 1932). Rumour spreading shows such characteristics. And so does the representation of new ideas. They are subject to the predominance of assimilation over accommodation.

Unless the contribution of the rule theorists continues to be developed and spelt out in its full complexity and in precise detail, it may die as a result of people extracting a false version of it. The complementary hazard is that people will not be willing to invest the intellectual effort to comprehend the complexity that will emerge, but that will be their loss.

The Ontogenesis
of Speech Acts
JEROME BRUNER

It has become increasingly customary in the past several decades to consider language as a code, a set of rules by which grammatical utterances are produced and in terms of which they are comprehended in order to extract their meaning. This tradition, ancient in origin, was greatly reinforced by the brilliant insights of de Saussure (1916) and Jakobson (1972), amplified by Chomsky (1965). It has resulted in stunning perception of the formal nature of language and has permitted the application of powerful mathematical techniques to the field of linguistics. But all advances in knowledge have attendant costs. Depth of insight must often be earned at the cost of breadth of perspective. So, whilst we have in the past decades learned much about the *structure* of language, we have perhaps overlooked important considerations about its *functions*. Our oversight has, I think, turned our attention away from how language is used. And since the uses of language are, I believe, crucial to an understanding of how language is acquired, how it is *initially* used, the study of language acquisition has been distorted. That distortion has, of course, been in the direction of a preoccupation with syntax, an emphasis on the changing structure of language. It is a preoccupation whose results have hopefully purged us of simple-minded accounts of language acquisition as a gradual process of storing up reinforcements or associations or imitations. But language is acquired as an instrument for regulating joint activity and joint attention. Indeed, its very structure reflects these functions and its acquisition is saturated with them.

Because I should like to emphasise function in what follows, I think of the present exercise as a study in the ethology of language acquisition in the human infant. Such an emphasis may lead us, with less mystery, better to understand how the young of our species are able in so startlingly short a time to master a language of such structural complexity that its rules still defy in large measure complete formal analysis. What may be innate about language acquisition is not *linguistic* innateness, but some special features of human action and human attention that permit language to be decoded by the uses to which it is put. This assertion, I hope to show, is not as circular as it may at first seem.

I shall begin by considering briefly what is intended by 'speech acts' in contrast with the more usual units for analysing language, and then turn to a consideration of certain possible correspondences that may exist between the nature of actions and the structure of speech used by speakers both to represent these actions and to involve others in them. This may suggest how a knowledge of the requirements of action may help in 'cracking the linguistic code'.

The second part of the paper is concerned with a brief analysis of language acquisition, strongly influenced by several recent studies, empirical and theoretical alike.[1] All of them represent a sharp break with the approach to language acquisition that reached its peak in the mid-1960s, an approach dominated by the formalism of Chomsky (1965); the break being well represented by Bloom's monograph (1971) and by Brown's masterful monograph (1973). It will provide a benchmark about the state of our knowledge about language acquisition.

Finally, we shall consider briefly the beginnings of a study of the transition from pre-linguistic to linguistic communication in infants, now in progress in Oxford—more in the interest of illustrating a concrete approach to speech acts and their ontogenesis than of drawing conclusions. The approach, as already noted, is premised on the view that language is a specialised and conventionalised extension of co-operative action. To be understood properly its acquisition must be viewed as a transformation of modes of assuring cooperation that are prior to language, prior both phylogenetically and ontogenetically, though the present paper deals only with the latter.

1. See Brown, 1973; Nelson, 1973; Ryan, 1973; Schlesinger, 1974; Sugarman, 1973; Reynolds, 1976; Greenfield & Smith, 1976; Dore, in press

Language in Psychological Perspective

Let me begin by outlining briefly the view of language that has been developed over the past decade by a group of philosophers who were, I think, clearing the ground for a pragmatically oriented study of language: Austin (1962), Grice (1968), Strawson (1959) and Searle (1970), principally. Their aim as analytic philosophers was, of course, to examine the way in which ordinary language is used, and I emphasise *used*. The tradition stems, probably, from Wittgenstein's sibylline maxim that the meaning of an utterance is its use. These philosophers insisted that there are at least *two* ways of conceiving of meaning in language. One of them is in terms of the actual utterance, without regard either for the context in which uttered or for the objective of the utterer in addressing the discourse to another. The second approach considers, not the utterance in a timeless sense, but, to use Grice's phrase, in relation to its occasion of use. This is the *utterer's meaning*, and it cannot be judged in terms of truth or falsity conditions or by well-formedness in the light of grammatical rules, but rather in terms of its effectiveness in achieving the speaker's intention, or some other outcome. Effectiveness, of course, will depend upon the speaker's capacity to use the conventions and rules of the subculture in which the utterance occurs (see Grice, 1976), his sense of the appropriateness of the utterance to the situation. Searle remarks that the criterion by which such utterances might be judged, instrumental to their effectiveness, is felicity. The request, 'Would you be so kind as to pass the salt?' is not a request for information about the listener's limits of compassaion, but an utterance that follows the convention of leaving a potential donor an apparent option in fulfilling a request, in order that the utterance be not interpreted as a command. Whatever the grammatical structure of the utterance, it is encoding a convention of request that the speaker must understand in some simpler, *non-linguistic* way before he is likely to comprehend or to use such utterances appropriately. The relation between the instrumental or illocutionary function of an utterance and its grammatical structure is, I shall argue later, crucial to language acquisition. It is the interplay between the two that permits the child to enter the language so quickly. We shall examine this matter in more concrete detail later.

What is implied by this assertion is, of course, that from a psychological point of view the formal structure of language is by no means totally arbitrary (Hockett, 1963).[2] We shall illustrate two crucial ways in which the structure of language may be in very good correspondence with the psychological events and processes that it must encode. These instances are offered to explore the hypothesis that early language, to be acquired, must reflect the nature of the cognitive processes whose output it encodes. One instance has to do with the isomorphism between a central lingustic form, predication, and the nature of human attention processing. The second is the relationship between linguistic case structure and the organisation of action. While predication and case structure are here offered as instances of a general rule, they are taken to be central to the issue of language acquisition.

Concerning predication, I refer to the topic-comment structure of utterances, reflected formally in such devices as subject-predicate in grammar or as function and arguments in logical analysis. Topic-comment structure reflects an underlying feature of attention, as I shall try to indicate, and its realisation in language by the use of subject-predicate rules is sufficiently akin to this characteristic of attention to make these rules easily accessible to a language learner. As Chomsky (1965 : 221) notes, 'It might be suggested that Topic-Comment is the basic grammatical relation of surface structure corresponding (roughly) to the fundamental Subject-Predicate relation of deep structure', and he goes on to comment that 'often, of course, Topic and Subject will coincide'.

All natural languages exhibit topic-comment structure, with varied devices for representing topics and for commenting upon them. Subject-predicate constructions, for example, are universal (Greenberg, 1963 : 59). But note also the flexibility of topicalisation, the ability of language to group together previously diverse referents and to unify them into a single new topic upon which comment can then be made. Such topicalisation, again, corresponds to phenomena of regrouping and reorganisation in perceptual attention and in reorganisation in memory recall. There may be a stronger version of this general point. Greenberg (1963) proposes as his first universal of languages that 'In declarative sentences with nominal subject and object, the dominant order is almost always one in which the subject precedes the object'. He then goes on to note, 'The order of elements in language parallels that in physical experience or the order of knowledge',

2. Jakobson (1963) argues that one finds a very high incidence of grammatical universals when one uses semantic criteria for defining them and that the semantic mapping of the universe could not, accordingly, be arbitrary.

using as example the universal order 'implying → implied'. 'No one thinks to write a proof backwards' (: 61). We do not propose Greenberg's stronger form, that topic and comment, being experienced in that order, are represented linguistically in the same order, but mention it here in preparation for taking it up in a later section.

If one were to sum up the past decade of work on attention in a few words, it is that attention is a feature extracting routine in which there is a steady movement back and forth between selected features and wholes. Neisser (1967) has characterised the process as analysis-by-synthesis, a process of positing wholes (topics) to which parts or features or properties may be related and from which the new wholes may be constructed. The predicational rules of natural language are surely a well-adapted vehicle for expressing the results of such attentional processing: topic-comment structure in language permits an easy passage from feature to its context and back, while topicalisation provides a ready means for regrouping new sets of features into hypothesised wholes to be used as topics on which to comment'

Indeed, studies of visual attention by the use of the recording of eye-movements suggest how parallel is the structure of topic-comment in language and in visual inspection. In work by Mackworth and Bruner (1970), where the subjects have the task of identifying a picture emerging from blur, one sees a mixed pattern of large eye-movements (in search of overall integration into a topic or 'subject') and small saccades searching out detailed features for use in checking and commenting. And the language by which subjects report their hypotheses parallels the process so closely that it is hard to resist the impression that one was designed for the other—either in a Whorfian fashion, with scanning reflecting sentence requirements, or in our sense, of language conforming to the processing pattern of perceptual attention. It is worth noting, by the way, that one of the aspects of visual scanning that develops greater flexibility between age five and adulthood is just this deployment of large and small saccades—knowing when to go from part to whole and back.

As for the possible isomorphism between grammatical structure and the structure of action, I have in mind here the fundamental case-grammatical form of language, the presence in *all* languages of categories of agent, action, object of action, recipient of action, location, possession, etc. Grammatical categories might, after all, have been universally mindful of such distinctions as whether experience comes from within or from without, or whether situations are under control or out of control, or whether we are dealing with allies or those opposed to us. In fact, few languages have such primary grammatical markings though they can all handle such distinctions indirect by propositional means. The *primitive* categories of grammar refer rather to *actions* as carried out by *agents* and having *effects* of particular *kinds* in particular *places*, etc. And these categories, as we shall see, are of particular importance in the early acquisition of language. It is quite beside the point here that linguists have raised serious doubts about Fillmore's (1968) effort to give such case grammar the status of a generative base structure for adult speech. From the psychologist's point of view, the seeming isomorphism of action categories and case grammatical ones requires close scrutiny for what it suggests about how language is first used, and therefore how it is acquired.

We shall try to illustrate later some examples of how this correspondence between case grammar and the structure of joint action carried out by infant and caretaker aid the former in acquiring a starting grammar. For the infant first learns pre-linguistically to make the conceptual distinctions embodied in case grammar and, having mastered privileges of occurrence in action sequences in which these distinctions are present, begins to insert non-standard signals that mark the distinctions. Initially, of course, the context is sufficient for the mother to interpret the child's intentions—to supply the grammar, so to speak. In time, and by substitution, the signalling becomes more conventional and can be comprehended with less contextual support. It is, as we shall see, much closer to the picture set forth long ago by DeLaguna (1927) than to the structural descriptions of how syntactic knowledge differentiates out of innate knowledge of linguistic universals. What is universal is the structure of human action in infancy which corresponds to the structure of universal case categories. It is the infant's success in achieving joint action (or the mother's success, for that matter) that virtually leads him into the language. In this sense, mastery of 'utterer's meaning'—effectiveness or felicity in achieving ends—provides the child with a conceptual structure that is also embodied in the language he is to learn.

Mutual Action, Shared Attention and Language Acquisition

In his 1970 book (with which he now no longer quite agrees, see McNeill, 1974), David McNeill began his discussion of the acquisition of language with the bold assertion: 'The facts of language acquisition could not be as they are unless the concept of a sentence is available to children at the start of their learning.' The child's efforts, says McNeill, 'can be viewed as a succession of hypotheses that a child adopts concerning the form sentences take in the language around him'. I would substitute for this claim a more credible one, that follows from what has been said: 'The facts of language acquisition could not be as they are unless fundamental concepts about action and attention are available to children at the beginning of learning.' I should add to this, perhaps, the proviso that these concepts must be ones that are developed in mutuality with a speaker of the language. But we may postpone consideration of this latter point until later when the process of acquisition is treated.

Support for the general proposition comes from the meagre but growing stock of universals characterising language acquisition. Melissa Bowerman (1970) has examined acquisition data for semantic relations in Finnish, Luo, English and Samoan grammatical forms in early Stage I with MLUs between 1.3 and 1.5 morphemes. I shall use modified terms for them, differing somewhat from hers. They are:

1. Agent-action (e.g. Mommy push)
2. Action-object (e.g. Bite finger)
3. Possession (e.g. Aunt car)
4. Demonstrative marker (e.g. There cow)
5. Feature marker (e.g. Big bed)
   (Semi-universals)
6. Location marker
      object (e.g. Car garage)
      action (e.g. Sit bed)
7. Negation
8. Recurrence (e.g. More nut)
9. Greeting notice (e.g. Hi spoon)

In later Stage I, MLU up to 2.0, the following is universal:

10. Recipient of action-experience (e.g. Show me book, or Hear horn).

Roger Brown (1973) notes that the first three observed in the children he has examined are *agent-action*, *action-object*, and *agent-object*, part

realisations of the triad *agent-action-object*. The initial semantic operations he has observed are *nomination, non-existence, recurrence, location,
possession*, and *attribution*.

Observing the way in which children at an earlier stage combine
their *single-word* holophrases with actions or gestures, Greenfield and
Smith (1976) report a similar list of relations even prior to these
simple sentences. Schlesinger (1974) interprets the first-appearing
relations found by Greenfield *et al.* as broadening and differentiating
the child's conceptual range for dealing with agents, actions, and
objects of actions. The first eight are as follows:

Vocative	'Mommy', when requiring something
Object of demand	'Milk', while reaching for it
Action performed by agent	'Gone', when mother leaves him
Inanimate object of action	'Spoon', when mother takes out spoon
Action of inanimate object	'Gone', after mother says 'The record is up there'
Affected person (or recipient of action)	'Mommy', when giving her something
Agent of action (or instrumental agent)	'Mommy', handing knife to mother after trying unsuccessfully to cut with it

These various sets of data suggest that the child, in using language
initially, is very much oriented toward pursuing (or commenting upon)
action being undertaken jointly by himself and another. This includes
not only agent, action, and object, but also control, as represented by
possession. Part of that preoccupation involves calling attention to
objects and people involved in that process—nomination, demonstrative marking, non-existence, greeting, location. And another part
involves commenting upon what is attended to, as in feature marking.

Are there any special difficulties involved in inferring that the child
himself 'has' intentions and the he infers intentions in others? For both
are implied in the claim that the child understands the distinctions in
the relations *agent–action–object–recipient*. I think not. We may infer
intention by the usual criteria of direction, terminal requirements,

substitution of means, persistence, etc. (c.f. Bruner, 1974). And, we shall see, there is sufficient systematic behaviour for inferring that the child can distinguish his own agency from that of another—surely implied by negativism before ever negation is realised linguistically. The inference is, as noted, on systematic response in the child, much as in judging whether a subject 'has' any other form of concept (Bruner, Goodnow, and Austin, 1956).

The one thing that is special about the kinds of concepts the child is said to be operating with is that they are based on the presumption that the child grasps the 'idea' of intersubjectivity—that others have intentions. Does this not run counter to Piagetian ideas about decentration? A full discussion of this issue will surely take us too far afield, but a few points can be made to clarify it. For one thing, there is ample evidence available that the child in his responses from a few weeks of age distinguishes the category of people from the category of things (Trevarthen, 1974) and shows distinctive responses to each. There is also abundant evidence, reviewed by Robson (1967), that there is a distinctive response in the infant to eye-to-eye contact and that it is a crucial bonding phenomenon between infant and caretaker. Moreover, smiling and vocalisation can be greatly increased in the infant by like responses in an adult, as we know from studies by Brackbill (1967) and Rheingold, Gewirtz and Ross (1959). A series of new studies by Maratos (1973), Mounoud (personal communication, 1973), and Meltzoff (personal communication, 1974) indicates that the infant in the opening weeks of life can imitate facial and manual gestures in an adult—though he obviously cannot 'see' his own reactions (at least in the case of facial imitation). And we shall examine in somewhat more detail later observations in our own study indicating that as early as four months of age, the infant will follow an observer's line of regard.

This is not to say that the child is born equipped with a 'finished conceptual schema' for interpreting intersubjective phenomena—that he 'knows about' sharing experience with another from the start, or knows about anothers' intentions. Rather, it is to say that the child has the innate capacity to construct such schemata. He does so by interpreting feedback from another as constituting a special class of events—'intersubjective' events in contrast to other events. And he is greatly aided in this by the existence of systematic intentional (or intention-like!) behaviour in the people with whom he comes in contact.

From Pre-linguistic Concepts to Language

How precisely does the child's knowledge of action and how does his way of attending lead him to grasp concepts embodied in language? The Piagetian formulation of internalisation and symbolisation of action schemas is suggestive (e.g. Sinclair, 1969) but rather too vague to be satisfactory, though it points in a promising direction. The more specific question is how, for example, do concepts of agents, actions, objects, recipients, etc., grasped presemantically aid the child in learning the communicative devices that encode these concepts? Or, similarly, how does mastery of joint reference prelinguistically lead the child to grasp such devices as topic-comment predication and demonstratives? We consider some processes briefly now in order to suggest possible ways of looking at illustrative data in the final section.

A first process involves the infant in the learning of the segments of joint action with the mother—their *positions* or *privileges of occurrence* in sequences involving agent–action–object and recipient. The child is not only learning to distinguish the segments but also learning substitution rules, learning to reverse order (so that the recipient of action, the child, begins to trade positions with the agent) in what must be an early example of deixis. In time, the child learns distinctive, if nonstandard ways of signalling different segments of the action-sequence. Finally, standard communication is substituted for these. These are matters that can be observed in detail, and below we will consider some examples.

A second process comes from the elaborate construction of routines for assuring joint reference. At the outset, probably, the process begins with innate support through eye-to-eye contact—an exchange of attention between addresser and addressee whose *general* importance is probably overrated though its special role for establishing 'intersubjectivity' may be crucial. More striking still, at least to me, is the speed with which mother and infant follow each other's line of regard and come to attend jointly to common, concrete foci. Collis and Schaffer (1975) have written recently of the mother's tendency to follow the child's line of regard and to comment upon what the child is thought to be observing. Scaife in my laboratory has indeed found (1974) that even at four months the child (given undistracting conditions) also follows the mother's line of regard, and soon after does so more readily when the mother's phonation is of the pattern of such demonstratives as *Oh look!* In time, this primitive cycle is replaced by a simple semanticity—things have labels and uttering the label becomes a manoeuvre in establishing joint reference—particularly in the context of joint action (c.f. Brown and Berko, 1960). Often, labelling, under these circumstances, serves as a vocative or command as well.

Once attention is jointly directed, as we shall see, the mother will systematically act upon or comment upon what has caught their joint attention. The routine 'attend to → act upon' is a highly practical one. It readily sets up an expectancy of order: locus-feature or object-name or object-act. Or to quote Greenberg (1963) again, 'The order of elements in language parallels that in physical experience or the order of knowledge'. It is a point that Cromer (1974a) makes much of and one that Brown also notes in pointing to the importance of order in the early grammatical utterances of the child. Cromer (1974b) has found that action is always imputed to the subject of a sentence even when it is of the kind 'John is easy to bite', rather than 'John is eager to bite'. By the same token, Slobin (1966) has reported for a highly inflected language like Russian, children first learn order rules about permissible sequences of subject-verb-object before they learn the inflected, adult form of language.

A fourth process is puzzling. It consists of the child learning phonological patterns almost as place holders, imitatively. They constitute, even preverbally, a kind of prosodic envelope or matrix into which the child 'knows' that morphemes go—an interrogative and a vocative/demand contour, and possibly an indicative. It is as if mode were being inferred, a place holding matrix established, and lexis then added. It is a point John Dore (in press) makes much of. There is the possibility that distinctive 'speech acts' are learned in a primitive fashion by this means—demand prosody involving a rising intonation, etc. There is little concrete evidence save the often repeated observation that prosodic patterns come to set up definite expectancies in the child and that the child not only 'comprehends' intention in these patterns, but learns to produce them intentionally as well.

But these illustrative processes only account for the start. There is something more that leads the child toward elaborating rule structures in communication. I think such elaboration is inherent in play, particularly in the mutual play between mother and infant. In virtually all of our own records, as we shall see, elaborative play is a major feature of early mother-infant interaction—involving complex role shifting between partners as with *Peekaboo* and exchange and also ritualised and repeated play on objects, as with pushing a ball back and forth. In such play there is not only accentuation of the agent–action–object axis of the child's enterprises but also the development of signalling and sequencing rules. There is a crucial point here. *It is that play has the effect of drawing the child's attention to communication itself, and to the structure of the acts in which communication is taking place.* It is a point that has been made recently by several writers, and I have argued it myself at some length in a recent paper (1972). As Elkonin (1971) puts it, 'Just as the mastery of objective reality is not possible without formation of activity with objects, exactly in the same manner is language mastery not possible without formation of activity with language as the material object . . .' (: 141). For Elkonin, play is the species-specific mode of dealing with language and its rules as the object of attention. It is perhaps Peter Reynolds who analyses the operation of this process most precisely. As Cazden (1973) paraphrases his argument, 'According to Reynolds, all behaviour can be classified into discontinuous 'affective-behavioural systems'.' Play is one such system, an inevitable part of the developmental process, with very special characteristics. In Reynolds' words:

> The playfulness of an act does not pertain to what is done but to the way it is done (: 4–6) . . . Play possesses no instrumental activity of its own. It derives its behaviour patterns from other affective-behavioural systems. (: 12)
> In play, behaviour, while functioning normally, is uncoupled (and buffered) from its normal consequences. . . . Therein lies both the flexibility of play and its frivolity. (: 7)
> Behaviour patterns are elaborated and integrated in play but are returned to non-play affective behaviour system control for utilitarian execution. (: 12)

In the play mode, segments of behaviour are converted to non-utilitarian purposes—especially to signalling, to substitution and variation, etc. The rituals of play become the objects of attention, rather than being instrumental to something else.

In a word, it is with the buffering of action from its consequences that the child begins to elaborate his signalling in action situations, trying out variations, searching for varied orders of combining acts and signals. And it is at this point that the mother's constant interpretations of the child's intended meanings become so crucial in confirming the child's hypotheses.

With this much before us, we may now turn to some examples from a pilot study.

Some Illustrations

We take some illustrations from a pilot study of six infants, seen about fortnightly for about six months from approximately seven months of age.[3] Infants and mothers came to our laboratory where a home-like room had been constructed. From time to time observations were also made at the homes of our subjects. All sessions were video-taped. We sampled three forms of behaviour in which communication might develop: we arranged to have mothers feed their infants, to give them a bath, and to 'play those games with their children that they were both enjoying most these days'. All of the children began with no conventional language. All of them had some holophrases when we finished.

Our object was to explore the manner in which joint enterprises grew up between mother and infant, how these became elaborated, and how language and other less standard forms of communicating entered the scene. The objective of the data gathering was to collect not so much a corpus of utterances to be analysed, but rather to trace the development of various forms of action contexts so that we could ascertain the manner in which communication entered and altered them. This, in effect, is the method that is imposed by the theoretical view being proposed here. At that, it was not 'successful' in the methodological sense, since there was too little 'standardisation' imposed on the kinds of episodes that could occur in the course of feeding, bathing, and playing with an infant. In our current work we are imposing a somewhat closer control on the kinds of joint enterprises we record—exchanges, calls for aid, disappearance—reappearance games, etc. But control, we find, must be tempered by a sense of opportunity if the observation sessions are not to be made stilted or forced.

The first and most evident thing to be observed was the ubiquitousness of the mother's interpretations of the child's actions, almost inevitably taking the form of inferring the baby's intentions or other

3. I wish to express my thanks to Miss Wendy Zerin and to Miss Virginia Sherwood for help in these observations and also to Dr. Aidan Macfarlane and Mr. John Churcher for aid in recording. Dr. Michael Scaife and Dr. Renée Paton have also helped in the analysis of data.

directive states. I am entirely in agreement with Nelson (1973) and
Ryan (1974) that an enormous amount of consequent behaviour flows
from the nature of these interpretations. Interpretations seem to be
principally of two types, some mothers tending to favour one more
than the other. One form is an interpretation of the infant's behaviour
as an intention to carry out some action. In such instances, mothers most
often see their role as supporting the child in achieving an intended
outcome, entering only to assist or reciprocate or 'scaffold' the action.
'Scaffolding' refers to the mother's effort to limit, so to speak, those
degrees of freedom in the task that the child is not able to control—
holding an object steady while the child tries to extract something from
it, screening the child from distraction, etc.

A second mode of interpretation is more concerned with attention
than with action: the child is not so much trying to *do* something as he
is trying to *find out about something*. An obvious instance is showing
something to the child, handing him an object he is looking at that is
out of reach, turning one's gaze to where the child is looking, or getting
the child to look at what catches the mother's interest. In its more
advanced form, this type of aid spills over into naming objects or
parts of the body or segmentable actions.

We early observed that mothers seek themselves to 'standardise'
certain forms of joint action with the child—mostly in play but also in
earnest. This usually consists of setting up standard action formats by
which the child can be helped to interpret the mother's signals, her
gestures, her intentions. They are recurrent occasions that provide the
child an opportunity of predicting not only the mother's intentions
but, so to speak, to calibrate his attention with hers. These episodes
also permit the child to develop more or less standard ways of signalling
his intent, whether it be to refer to an object or to signal some desire.
At this stage of development in communication, the establishment of
illocutionary effectiveness is paramount, the object being to develop
means for operating with mutual consent.

In the case of intention-oriented interactions, the principal form of
signalling is *marking the segments of action*. Most usually it begins by the
use of terminal marking, the use of what might be called a *completive*.
The child takes a mouthful of newly introduced food from a spoon;
the mother exclaims, '*Good boy!*' with distinctive intonation. Or he
offers back an object handed to him, and the mother exclaims '*There!*'
Or he removes a ring from a peg-and-ring toy, and the mother cries
'*Aboom!*' It may well be that completion marking of this kind serves as

an initial step in primitive semantic segmentation, the forming of units. Greenberg (1963) notes at least three linguistic universals that relate to emphasis on marking not the beginning but the end of utterances, a 'general tendency to mark the ends of units rather than the beginnings'. He remarks, 'This is probably related to the fact that we always know when someone has just begun speaking but it is our sad experience that without some marker we don't know when the speaker will finish' (: 81). The same, of course, can be said for action patterns when two are involved when there is need to signal that one member, in this case the mother, regards the act as completed. The notable thing about video records of young children's behaviour is that, in fact, they are so continuous, so 'seamless' and without definite beginnings and ends. The use of completives provides a finite structure that permits reproducibility. And reproduction there is, for it would seem as if both infant and mother take particular pleasure in repeating acts (with variation) for which a definite completive has been agreed upon.

Segments of action are, in effect, positions occupied in a sequence by varying or substitutable acts. It is in this sense that we conceive of them as representing privileges of occurrence for classes of acts and, consequently, a particularly important form of psycholinguistic learning. We shall consider this matter of substitution within position later.

At the outset, in this process, the mother is almost always the agent of the action, the child the recipient or 'experiencer'. His mode of signalling for the recurrence of the action is usually to show a typical level of excitement or a generalised vocative in an appropriate context, or by performing some portion of the desired action (e.g. pumping up and down on the adult's knee to produce a recurrence of 'Ride a Cock-horse'). The focus is upon mother-as-agent. Typically, mothers then seek to dissociate act from agent, and they follow a surprisingly regular pattern. It consists of dramatising or idealising the act itself with some kind of serial marking. Handing the child a desired object, the mother will move it slowly toward him with an accompanying sound increasing in pitch or loudness as it approaches the child, or changing sounds with steps in the approach. Over a period of days this will be repeated as a game, until the child begins to show an anticipatory act, usually at the end of the approach, taking hold of the object rather than having it placed before him. In the process, the agent and the act are being differentiated, attention shifting from the former to the latter. The child next becomes the agent in a reciprocal process of handing the object back to the mother, the mother becoming the recipient of the action. During this development the child's orientation to the mother changes, with a differentiation of when she is oriented toward object or action (line of regard directed at locus of event), and when she is oriented toward agent (line of regard toward mother's face). The following record is typical. It is from one of our six subjects, Ann, on whom we shall concentrate in this account to provide the necessary continuity. The Mother (M) and the Child (C) are handling a small object back and forth. The first episodes noted occurred when Ann was 9 months, 2 weeks.

Phase I. C has picked up a block. Looks at M, then down at block and holds it up to M. M puts out her hand to take it and C, looking at her hand, withdraws the object. (M says 'no?') C then looks at the block and plays with it. After a few seconds, C looks at M's hand again, lies the block in it, without releasing. Still looking at M's hand, withdraws the object.

[In our method of scoring, we infer that when C treats M as recipient of action, rather than as agent, C looks at M's hand or attends to her act of receiving, rather than looking at her eyes or face. The alternative modes of responding are contained in the following sequences in which the pattern alters.]

Phase II. (Several minutes later.) C looking at block on floor when M stretches out her hand. C looks at it and, keeping gaze fixed on M's hand, then: waves object about with vocalisation; takes hold of M's hand with her right and, still holding it, lies the block in M's hand with her left (M says 'thank you'); withdraws block. C then looks back to the block as she releases M's hand.

[We believe that C continues to treat M as a recipient of action, forcing M to acquiesce by 'physical restraint'. Attention is still to her hand rather than *en face*.]

Phase III. (Give-and-take, C never releasing the object, has preceded.) C looks at M and presents O. M takes it, despite C's attempts to retain hold, and puts it slightly behind her. C looks at floor, then at M, and reaches to M with vocative cry. M presents the object and C takes it, looking at it. C then 'hugs' the object and looks at M.

[Note that M is now becoming a fellow agent and C, after having been agent, becomes recipient of the same act.]

Phase IV. (Age 11 months, 2 weeks. M & C sitting on floor, playing with plastic shapes.) C picks up square, looks at M and

hands to her with vocalisation. M takes, saying 'thank you'. C
looks down, picks up another square & holds up to M, looking at
her hand. M takes with 'thank you'. M closes hand, covering
objects. Looking at M's hand, C tries to pry squares and failing,
picks up & then drops a ring on the floor. Again reaches for
objects in M's hand, looking at it. M releases; C takes first square
and looks at it; looks at hand again and takes second square,
vocalising; drops second square and looks down.

[Note that M has prevented a truly reciprocal agency from
developing by making it more difficult for the child to regain
possession (i.e. the format C give, M take, C reach for, M give,
C take does not occur). In this new situation, C once again
dominates the role of agent. Note also, however, the child's
increased awareness of M as a *possible* fellow agent.]

The next set of episodes starts with Ann at the same age. She has
begun to signal in the exchange routine but only for giving, using *Kew*.
This conforms to the use of a completive as the earlier marker. In
three months, the demonstrative *Look* has replaced *Kew* in the giving
phase, and *Kew* has moved into its correct receiving position in the
sequence. Ann has learned the correct serial order in the act—which was
not an easy matter, as we can see from the first episode—and also the
correct privileges of occurrence in the discourse for the accompanying
vocalisations of by now quite standard lexical items.

(Nine months, two weeks) Give-and-take game. C offers book to
M and then withdraws it when M reaches for it, with C showing
great excitement. Hands book to M, saying *Kew* when M takes it.
    (Ten months, two weeks) C plays with blocks. Says *Kew* when
offering block to camera operators. Not observed ever to say *Kew*
when receiving block or any object. Give-and-take game always
involves Ann saying *Kew* when handing block to M.
    (Twelve months, two weeks) M hands C ring. Now C says *Kew*
when receiving. Three minutes later C hands M toy postbox, a
favourite. C says *Look* when handing.

Note one additional thing about this series of exchanges. Initially,
Ann must learn to deal with deixis in an action situation; shifting from
the role of recipient of an action to being the agent of the action with
the previous agent as recipient, and back again. In learning to distin-

guish the positions of *Kew* and *Look*, a form of linguistic deixis is mastered, not unlike the later distinction between *I* and *you* to be used differentially depending upon whether uttered by ego or other. Note also, in passing, that there is no effort to correct on the part of the mother. We would agree with Nelson (1973) that it is often the case that mother's correction of a 'mismatch' inhibits the interchange— perhaps by destroying the playfulness earlier commented upon as so crucial to language exchanges.

The next set of episodes involving Ann relate to Peekaboo, and relate to appearance/disappearance and its variation. I present it to give some sense of the substitution rules that enter into the exchanges and the kinds of variations that enter as well.

Ann first shows interest in appearance and disappearance at an early session, at nine months. She is looking at a picture book, characteristically fingering pictures. She closes and then opens the book to pictures, and repeats several times, looking at mother at close and at open, mother responding by smiling and raising eyebrows in recognition. Then Peekaboo emerges at eleven months.

> (Eleven months) M initiates game while drying C's hair after bath, covering baby's face with towel, saying *boo* twice on uncovering. Both laugh. Ten minutes later, C initiates, raising her petticoat over face and holding there until M says *boo*. Laughs and lowers petticoat. C repeats three times, M maintaining excitement by varying time to say *boo*, and C does not lower until signal *boo* is given.
>
> (Eleven months and two weeks) C has cleaning tissue in hand. Raises it in two hands to cover face. Says *Achoo*, lowers, and looks at M, both laughing. M repeats on herself, saying *Achoo*.

Closer analysis of both episodes shows that before game in both instances, initiator is eye-to-eye contact that is steady and more than glance. Similar eye-to-eye contact after unmasking.

Note about the format of the game that there is an agentive position that is subject to substitution (C and M both act as hiders and unmaskers); that an instrumental, the hiding screen, is varied; that the unmasking signal is not only varied, but that the variation is context sensitive with a cleaning tissue evoking the variant call *achoo* (ordinarily used as a completive by the mother when wiping the child's nose after a sneeze); and that, finally, there is an expected duration of hiding that is varied. The episodes noted provide a striking example of the way in which, in play, a rule structure becomes elaborated. Indeed one is tempted to speculate concerning the role of phonological similarity in leading to the confabulation of *boo* and *achoo* in the Peekaboo format.

Finally consider an episode involving a topic-comment relationship, indicating the way in which a topic, *mouth*, becomes embedded in a matrix of related actions and referential episodes prior to the point at which it is given a name by the mother. The episodes extend from nine months to one year of age. By way of background, Ann and her mother had by nine months developed a ritual in which, in drinking from the cup, Ann acted as joint agent, mother waiting for Ann to join her hand to the cup before tilting it into a drinking position.

(Nine months) C holds cup to doll's mouth. Then puts cup to M's mouth who feigns drinking, this latter seven minutes after cup to doll episode.

(Same session, later) During nappy change, child holds toes up in air expecting game. M ostentatiously mouths and nibbles at C's toes. C laughs.

(Eleven months) Toes game has gone on at home. M asks, while drying C after bath, *Where are your toes?* C vocalises and laughs and holds legs high. M nibbles C's toes as in previous episode.

(Twelve months) M touches postbox with face on it and mouth for slot. C plays with it. Touches own mouth, pauses. Touches M's mouth, M responding by nibbling. Touches own mouth. Then comes a long vocalisation directed toward M. M says, *Yes, that's a mouth.*

Mouth, when it becomes a part of Ann's lexicon, is already connected with a range of contexts that provide comments that can at first be interpreted implicitly. But these contexts are, so to speak, placeholders that can themselves be labelled explicitly under appropriate conditions. The prior cognitive structure thus built up can serve, then, as a guide for decoding newly encountered properties of the lexicon and the grammar—as in such subject-verb construction as *mouth-bites* or *mouth-drinks* and *my-mouth* or *Mummy mouth*.

So much, then, for examples. They are all drawn from the period during which the child is first acquiring holophrases and combining them with action, gesture, and context to signal his intentions, to share attention with others, and to carry out joint enterprises. There is a very great step from this early acquisition to the point at which the child is able to handle communication by language alone, without dependence on context. A strong claim would be that the child comes to recognise the grammatical rules for forming and comprehending sentences by virtue of their correspondence to the conceptual framework that is constructed for the regulation of joint action and joint attention. This would be tantamount to saying that grammar originates as a set of rules abstracted from jointly regulated activity which has become codified in the culture of a linguistic community. Such a view would be not far removed from that set forth by Sinclair (1969) and is attractive in some ways.

It seems reasonable to suppose, however, that what we are discussing here is the child's initial entry into grammar, when it is still highly dominated by the addresser–addressee relationship and still very closely related to context. As Ullman (1963) notes in discussing the motivation of words at the semantic level, there has always been a conflict in linguistics between the 'naturalists' and the 'conventionalists', with the former looking to an intrinsic link between sound and sense, as in onomatopaeia or metaphor, and the latter invoking the principle of arbitrariness. He quite rightly points out that neither view could be entirely wrong. Our argument relates to the grammatical level more generally, particularly to a 'natural' semantic or pragmatic base for initial grammatical rules. The argument has been that the structures of action and attention provide benchmarks for interpreting the order-rules in initial grammar; that a concept of agent action object-recipient at the prelinguistic level aids the child in grasping the linguistic meaning of appropriately ordered utterances involving such case categories as agentive, action, object, indirect object, and so forth. And by the same token, a grasp of the topic-feature structure of shared experience aids the child in grasping the linguistic relation inherent in topic-comment and subject-predicate. The claim is that the child is grasping initially the requirements of joint action at a pre-linguistic level, learning to differentiate these into components, learning to recognise the function of utterances placed into these serially ordered structures, until finally he comes to substitute elements of a standard lexicon in place of the non-standard ones. The process is, of course, made possible by the presence of an interpreting adult who operates not so much as a corrector or reinforcer but rather as a provider, an expander, and idealiser of utterances while interacting with the child. It is not imitation that is going on, but an extension of rules learned in action to the semiotic sphere. Grammatical rules are learned by analogy with rules of action and attention.

In linguistic terms this accomplishment is highly exophoric, depending crucially on the context in which the communication occurs. Increasingly it becomes more context-free, more anaphorically sensitive to the rules of language themselves. There comes a point, as Cromer (1974a) notes, when the order of the elements in the utterance does not have to conform to the 'order of physical experience' and when intralinguistic rules come to be grasped directly and without being referred back to their conformity to experience. Yet, in looking even at skilled adult speech, we would do well to remember that language is full of 'hints' about how to proceed from sound to sense. But we should also bear in mind that joint experience and joint action are also full of hints as to how we should proceed from sense to sound. It is with this latter point that the present paper has been concerned.

Semantic Anthropology and Rules

PAUL HEELAS

. . . what I have said implies that social anthropology studies societies as moral, or symbolic, systems and not as natural systems, that it is less interested in process than in design, and that it therefore seeks patterns and not laws, demonstrates consistency and not necessary relations between social activities, and interprets rather than explains. These are conceptual and not merely verbal differences (Evans-Pritchard 1951 : 62).

Evans-Pritchard's vision of social anthropology stands in stark contrast to that held by many others, in particular Radcliffe-Brown. Broadly speaking, the difference is between anthropology viewed as the study of meaning, where social life is treated as a 'text' which has to be interpreted and analysed, and anthropology viewed as a branch of natural science, where social life is treated as a series of 'objects' whose relationships have to be established. The distinction can also be expressed as being between explanations that depend on the notion of following a rule and those that depend on the notion of causal determination.

In this paper I shall trace this opposition in connection with the anthropology of religion. Having introduced the distinction I shall then give some examples of how anthropologists of religion have employed the notion of a rule. In later sections my aim will be twofold: firstly to show an important explanatory limitation of the notion and secondly to demonstrate that the notion can be used to effect types of enquiry which cannot be performed within a causal or natural science framework.

To begin with, then, what are the more important differences between the study of religion as an attempt to establish causal connections and the study of religion as an attempt to discern the operation of rules? As the following table indicates, what I am treating as the social scientific approach rests on the assumption of methodological atheism.

Scientific (Positivistic) Enquiry	Semantic Enquiry
Methodological atheism	Methodological agnosticism
Correspondence view of truth emphasised	Coherence view of truth emphasised
Extra-religious explanations (involving scientifically accessible reality)	Intra-religious explanations (involving belief about religious realities)
Sociology of error	No sociology of error
Inductive/deductive procedures	Interpretative/deductive procedures
Causal theories (observer-articulated)	Rule portrayals (participant-based)

This is because the aim of the social scientist is to verify causal theories by testing them with respect to religious phenomena treated as a series of isolatable and measurable units, units which can yield empirical correlations. In other words, the social scientist cannot accept the religious tenet that God-talk is non-verifiable; that one is not entitled to apply scientific verificationist criteria to establish the truth value of assertions made about ultimate religious realities. So, in order to explain religious phenomena by relating them to a body of deductively linked theoretical elements, the social scientist has to 'relocate' ultimate religious realities. Only in this way—by arguing that gods and spirits are mental or social constructions—can he bring them within a scientifically accessible frame of reference.

Theological explanations involving non-verifiable, metaphysical assertions about ultimate religious realities are thereby avoided. But relocation has occurred. Beliefs about gods and spirits have become, in a manner of speaking, beliefs about society or whatever. It follows that participant-based, intra-religious understanding and explanation gives way to extra-religious styles of investigation. The social scientist, experimental psychologist or Freudian explains by reference to empirical realms which are typically non-religious and which result in projectionist-styled reductionism. An example of this may be found in Leach's remark that, for him, 'myths . . . are simply one way of describing certain types of human behaviour . . .' (1954 : 14). It also follows that a sociology or psychology of error is required. If, for example, one assumes that 'the god and the society are only one' (Durkheim, 1971 : 206), then one has to establish why participants have arrived at the deluded belief that their God really exists.

Because participant conceptualisations are not likely to involve extra-religious explanations containing accounts of error, the scientific investigator has to *establish* his causal or functional theories by proceeding inductively, discerning empirical generalisations or correlations, deducing from more general theories in order to attribute causal significance to the correlations, and then testing his theories. To rely solely on participant 'theories' and beliefs would appear to result in theology. Furthermore, a reliance on such beliefs would rule out the possibility of establishing causal relations. This is not simply because the beliefs are non-verifiable. More fundamentally, it is because, according to the oft-adopted Humean view of causality, causal generalisations necessarily have to do with contingent connections. Causal connections operate between antecedents and consequents which are separately identifiable. But participant theories and beliefs involve semantic and, as we shall see, rule-governed connections. One belief implies another, which means that they are not separately identifiable, and so are not open to causal analysis.

Causal connections differ from connections of meaning (or rule-governed connections) by virtue of the fact that only the former hinge on correlations between independent entities established by means of inductive techniques applied to empirical objects. A type of objectivity is involved in which phenomena are related according to theories, not simply according to what the phenomena might mean to participants (see Winch 1971 : 123–5). Thus the scientist cannot assume that thunder is related to lightning simply because participants happen to make a conceptual link between the two. The participants might be bad scientists or might not be being scientific at all.

Semantic anthropology is non-scientific in the sense that explanatory connections are established *via* the notion of rule rather than by applying causal theories. In the context of the anthropology of religion this involves adopting a position which Smart has referred to as methodological agnosticism (1973 : 54, 58). One proceeds *as if* religious entities exist in the fashion maintained by participants, thereby enabling one to engage in intra-religious explanation. This, in turn, focuses on the question of how beliefs cohere, not on how they correspond to, and can be verified in terms of, empirical reality. Thus the key to Evans-Pritchard's *Nuer Religion*, a classic of the semantic approach, is to be found in his remark that in the sense of 'the totality of Nuer religious beliefs and practices forming a pattern which excludes conflicting elements and subordinates each part to the harmony of the whole, we may speak of their religious system' (1956 : 318).

In elaborating why an emphasis on conceptual relationships and coherence leads to application of the notion of rule, we might consider Winch's observation that 'the notion of following a rule is logically inseparable from the notion of *making a mistake*' (1971 : 32). Rules can be followed or broken whereas stimuli are simply causally effective. If language use is a matter of using words in accordance with causal determinants, then it is difficult to see how one might offer a satisfactory account of how it is that we come to evaluate usage. It is difficult to explain both our capacity for making mistakes and our ability to recognise certain usages as mistaken. As Winch puts it, if the speaker did not think of language use in terms of correctness, a situation would arise in which everything he did would be as good as anything else he might do (: 32). Conceptual thinking is, however, not like this. Hence the applicability of the idea of rule. More generally, the meanings of words depend on their being correctly used. Grasping the meaning of a word involves assimilating the rules which regulate its use. In the absence of rules which ensure that participants use a word in the same way, speakers would not understand each other: the word could refer to anything.

In the semantic approach the examination of conceptual relations does not require repeated observations of the inductive type that occur in relation to causal theories. Semantic anthropology works with a participant-based conceptual objectivity rather than with the type of objectivity provided by the relocation procedure. Empirical inductions are not required because conceptual relationships are *given* by the meanings of words; they are given 'by definition'. Thus there is little or no point in establishing whether or not religious entities really exist from the point of view of a scientific standard. Such application of the correspondence theory of truth is largely irrelevant if one's task is to examine the conceptual relationships maintained by partici-

pants in order to determine the logic of how their concepts are related.[1]
An additional consideration is that establishing empirical correlations
often involves moving beyond the participant's frame of reference—
something which is of little value if one is examining participant-
based conceptual configurations. Central to the semantic approach to
conceptual configurations is an application of the notion of rule. It is
to the details of this that we now turn.

The analysis of ideational or cultural systems in terms of the notion of
rules can be shown to occur at two levels, the first involving rules and
the meanings of particular words, the second concerning the rationale
(or logical basis) of conceptual systems. The two levels are by no means
absolutely distinct, for understanding a particular word involves
grasping its relations with associated constructs. Nevertheless there are
differences. The first level involves what Ferre has called 'functional
analysis' (1970 : 91), the second a structural approach, where this is
broadly defined as 'fitting the pieces together to form a pattern'
(Leach, 1969 : 103).

Those who assume that meaning can best be understood in terms of
use or function have to recognise that rules of use often cannot be
clearly stated. Some rules are highly context-dependent; a word may
have many different meanings or functions depending on the context
in which it is used. I.A. Richards, in his brilliant and highly anthropological *Mencius on the Mind* (1964), argues for a new type of dictionary, a type based on the 'exercise of Multiple Definition' (: 92).
This technique involves listing significant usages of particular words and
then attempting to establish fundamental rules or criteria in order to
discriminate between different senses. However, although much useful
work can be done to this end, the approach has its limitations. For
example, granted that the meaning of the word 'taboo' is grasped once

1. Another way of putting this is in terms of Wittgenstein's remark, 'What has
to be accepted, the given, is—so one could say—*forms of life*' (1953 : 226). Methodological agnosticism fits with this emphasis on the 'given' (cf. Winch's use of such
terms as *a priori*, 'internal', and 'logical', and his argument that conceptual
relations are given by the meaning of words). It can also be noted that because
conceptual relations are 'given', interpretations cannot be verified by means of the
correspondence view of truth. It is because causal connections cannot be directly
deduced from participant beliefs that the scientist can apply the verification
principle. One reason why the semantic anthropologist cannot assess his interpretations in this way is that they do not lie far from participant conceptualisations.
So his criterion is that the greater the coherence he can find at the level of rules,
the more likely it is that his portrayal is correct (cf. Winch, 1967 : 18, and Evans-
Pritchard, 1956).

one has learnt to use it correctly, the fact remains that the rules which govern correct usage (rules which can be portrayed by describing contexts of use) may be extremely complex, ambiguous and vague. It may be the case that they cannot readily be formulated in such ways as, 'Word x should only be used in y contexts, and in all these instances it should be associated with z concepts'. Whereas grammatical rules tend to transcend contexts of use, semantic rules are embedded in specific circumstances.

Yet structural analysis of the type I am about to discuss aims to establish or discern general rules. It attempts to explicate the conceptual relations which link semantic items, the ultimate goal being the elucidation of the fundamental logical (or rational) principles of rules, together with the associated propositional (or conceptual) principles or rules, which constitute and regulate a particular system. Consider this in the context of the game of chess. The rules of chess have two aspects, constitution and regulation. They are constitutive in so far as they make the pieces what they are, and they are regulative in that the meaning of a piece entails that it be used in certain basic ways. One has to grasp what it is, for instance, for a piece to be a knight. One has to grasp the conceptual fit between how to move the knight and how to move other pieces. One also has to grasp the rules of check-mate and so forth. And if one is going to play well, one must learn the strategic implications of applying particular rules. What it is to make a move is conceptually related to the rules of the game and to the rules which constitute or regulate the reasoning activities involved in developing strategies. To examine the game of chess in structural terms is to portray the constitutive-regulative rules and the rationale of both these rules and the moves made with respect to them.

Clearly, it is not difficult to display and analyse the rationale of the basic propositional and rationale rules which constitute and regulate the game of chess. They can be explicitly formulated because they have been devised to form a closed, logically coherent system. In other words, one can state the rules and how they are related (their rationale) because the rules only apply in one context (that of the game). To varying degrees, the same applies in the context of ideational and cultural *systems.* Unlike the rules which are associated with a particular word when it is used in many contexts, the rules at work in cultural systems can be relatively easily explicated: granted a specific context of use, meaningful items will generally be related in a more or less limited number of ways.

The study of kinship has provided us with good examples of rule systems neatly formulated in logically coherent, structural form. Thus in the investigation of cross-cousin marriage, Needham has devised models to express the rationale largely embedded in appropriate kinship terminologies (1962 : 15). For various reasons, however, the anthropological study of religion has not produced many portrayals of analogous structural systems. Religious beliefs are often related according to vaguely defined contexts and according to such weakly rule-governed devices as metaphor. Another factor to be borne in mind is that religious systems frequently do not function in any simple sense as modes of knowledge or metaphysics. Many religions have at their core an inexpressible and, to use Otto's (1958) term, numinous reality. Beliefs then function to evoke a feeling-state which, as Ramsey (1957) has argued, results in considerable logical oddity.

I shall return to the question of conceptual principles in the context of the study of religion at a later point. For the present it is sufficient to note that rule systems have been established for some religious belief systems. For example, Evans-Pritchard has traced the rationale of what the Nuer mean when they say that a twin is *ran* (person) and that twins are *dit* (birds) (1956 : 128–33). He proceeds by assuming that a type of rationality is operative and by establishing relations among the relevant concepts, especially the concepts associated with normal human beings, twins, birds, height, and the Nuer God, *Kwoth*. The basic propositional rule which regulates this system can be formulated as, 'Kwoth is associated with everything on high, normal human beings with things of the earth'. This rule, it can be noted, is of the same order as equivalent rules in chess: it tells us that only a limited number of phenomena or 'moves' can be associated with particular semantic items or 'pieces'. Assuming that the Nuer case has rational properties, then the logical interplay between the basic rule and the basic constituent semantic items (beliefs about *Kwoth*, birds, and men) serves to order the system. Twins cannot strictly be of this earth because they are not like normal men. So they are *ran nhial* (persons of the above). And in this intermediary situation between *Kwoth* and the earth they occupy the same position as certain types of birds.

Another example is provided by the structural analysis of myth. In the light of what we have said about the difficulties of discerning rule systems in religious life, it is interesting that Lévi-Strauss has tended to steer clear of religious phenomena. But in the case of myth, as in such cases as 'twins are birds', he has supposed the logic to be sufficiently evident to permit structural analysis (see Lévi-Strauss, 1969 : 152). As a final example of the examination of religious phenomena in terms of rules, we can think of that tradition which has followed Durkheim and Mauss' idea that 'The first logical categories were social categories; the first classes of things were classes of men, into which these things were integrated' (1963 : 82). The theory as it appears in the work of much current anthropology, is that systems of social organisation (viewed largely in terms of structural properties) provide schemas for conceptualising phenomena to which they are only indirectly related. Thus Douglas' *Natural Symbols* (1970) is devoted to tracing and explaining types of fit between forms of social organisation/structure and forms of ritual/cosmological belief. She attempts to demonstrate, for instance, that in societies 'where social relations are structured to a minimal extent . . . the cosmos is experienced as benign, sufficiently to justify faith in the inner purity and goodness of the human individual' (: 103). She finds a correspondence between the strictly social and the strictly metaphysical, attributing this to the possibilities or constraints inherent in the patterns (or rules) of the social order. In this way her concern differs from Lévi-Strauss' preoccupation with the location of the basic 'rules', particularly those regulating classification, in the human mind.

Before turning to how anthropologists have used the notion of rule in the context of explaining social action, I should add that the type of structuralism adopted by Douglas and other contemporary anthropologists manages to combine the notion of rule (and thus the semantic approach) with a causal (and thus positivistic) approach. The approach involves deducing meanings and conceptual patterns from participant beliefs, and at least partly attributing such phenomena to scientific theories positing causal connections. The logic of this combination need not presently detain us. But we should note that the notion of rule apparently can operate in the context of reliance on the verification principle (Lévi-Strauss, 1963 : 10) and on the relocation procedure, which suggests that the distinction we have drawn between semantic and positivistic styles of inquiry is not always that easy to maintain.[2]

2. For example, conceptual analysis might uncover meanings similar to those that could be established, in a theory-dependent fashion, by a Durkheimian approach. However, this need not invalidate our distinction. Semantic enquiry does not involve theory-dependent meanings. Furthermore, it would not make the claim that sociological meanings are what the beliefs are really about, and so it would involve no sociology of error (see Evans-Pritchard, 1956 : 106–22; Bell, 1967 : 129).

I shall now examine some of the ways in which the notion of rule bears on the study of ritual and other forms of religious behaviour. A general discussion will be followed by a description of an illustrative case.

According to Winch, the analysis of meaningful behaviour is not qualitatively different from the analysis of cultural (or conceptual) relations. MacIntyre summarises Winch's position as follows:

> An action is *first* made intelligible as the outcome of motives, reasons, and decisions; and it is then made *further* intelligible by those motives, reasons and decisions being set in the context of the rules of a given form of social life. These rules logically determine the range of reasons and motives open to a given set of agents and hence also the range of decisions open to them. Thus Winch's contrast between explanation in terms of causal generalisations and explanations in terms of rules turns out to rest upon a version of the contrast between explanations in terms of causes and explanations in terms of reasons (1967 : 98–9).

This passage, emphasising as it does the regulative aspect of rules, is not entirely accurate. For Winch also makes the more fundamental claim that 'If social relations between men exist only in and through their ideas, then, since the relations between ideas are internal relations, social relations must be a species of internal relation too' (1971 : 123). In other words, Winch is claiming that even when someone cannot formulate a reason for his action the notion of rule is still relevant: the act has a sense and is internally related to other actions in that it commits the agent to behaving in certain ways in the future.

Winch also suggests that 'our language and our social relations are just two different sides of the same coin' (: 123). It follows that understanding and explaining actions is similar to understanding belief systems. But there is a qualitative difference, one which hinges on the importance of such notions as choice, motive and strategy for descriptions of action. A paradigm schema of action explanation is what is known as 'the means-end action schema' (see Parsons, 1968) or 'the logic of situation' approach (see Ryan 1970 : 177). Action generally involves the rational selection of means in order to attain ends. An individual acts as he does because he has applied his reasoning powers in the context of basic values or assumptions (e.g. 'I know I am an envious man') and circumstantial facts (e.g. 'I cannot easily be with the girl I love'). Rules enter into this kind of explanation in two ways. First, the rules of rationality are involved. And second, since the action is meaningful, it is related to other actions in a conceptual or internal fashion (i.e. to act in an envious fashion means that one cannot appropriately do certain things). Thus reasoning and acting involve social values, which can be portrayed as a rationale: being in love has a rationale because the values involved form a set which render certain actions appropriate and others inappropriate or misguided.

We have already introduced the argument that explanation of action cannot readily be construed in causal terms, but as it is an important and controversial issue it is worth elaborating. A favourite argument is that although beliefs and actions are not identical, actions are logically or internally related to beliefs rather than being contingently related. To believe in something means that if one is going to act one is going to act in certain ways. Acting meaningfully, as opposed to making a physical movement, is like making a statement: it must be interpreted in terms of reasons. As MacIntyre puts it, 'to explain the nod as a nervous tick is precisely to explain it not as something that I do, but as something that just happens' (1962 : 57). Then, as MacIntyre continues to argue, to explain the nod by introducing the reason that it is a response to a question is to introduce a state of affairs which involves rules rather than 'a generalization stating some constant conjunction which holds between questions and answers'. Rules are involved because the explanation, taking the form of a reason, has to do with a 'socially established and recognized practice, that of asking and answering questions'. To give another example, we learn to act morally by learning the meaning of a moral system, learning what various acts entail with respect to the system, learning how to justify our actions. We do not proceed by formulating theories to explain regularly observed conjunctions between beliefs and behaviour.

If the argument is correct, then the explanation of social action necessarily hinges on the notion of rule. That is, 'all behaviour which is meaningful (therefore all specifically human behaviour) is *ipso facto* rule-governed' (Winch, 1971 : 52). Consequently, the very basis of the positivistic approach is rendered out of place—observation followed by induction does not result in the establishment of rules and reasons (see MacIntyre, 1962 : 61; Waismann, 1965 : 121). But things are not as simple as I have made out. MacIntyre (1967) has since argued that reasons can be construed as causes, and many social scientists have in fact couched the logic of situation or methodological individualistic approach in the form of causal explanation (e.g. Jarvie, 1972).

In this connection it is interesting to note that there is one social scientific approach which escapes much of the controversy surrounding relationships between reasons and causes. This approach, sociological holism, differs from methodological individualism in that it does not treat the social process as a series of uniformities or regularities created by individuals acting in accordance with one another because they are reasoning about their activities in similar fashion. Instead, the individual is by-passed. The connections which are established hinge on inductive observations of action outputs, not on analysis of participant conceptualisations and reasons. One can correlate types of religious beliefs and types of social structure without introducing participant-based reasons. Indeed, precisely because such correlations are typically extra-religious, participant-based reasons and thus the rule approach are likely to be irrelevant to such pursuits.

We can now briefly examine the explanatory scope of the paradigm case of rule-governed accounts of social action, namely the means-end action schema. In some domains of social life the methodological individualist position appears to be useful. Barth has argued that by adopting it one can avoid the sociological holist mistake of treating behavioural patterns as the direct expression of normative rules (1966 : 1–3).[3] In his paper, 'The Analytical Importance of Transaction', he moves, so to speak, from the rules that constitute the game of chess to the study of the choices and strategies involved in playing a particular game: social patterns are taken to be 'the cumulative result of a number of separate choices and desisions made by people acting *vis-à-vis* one another' (1966 : 2). A similar approach has usefully been applied by Leach in his analysis of kinship and economics in the Ceylonese village of Pul Elyia (1961).

But what is suited to such domains as kinship and economics is not necessarily suited to religion. *Stratagems and Spoils* (1969), edited by Bailey, is about the rules of 'the social game' and how to win it. Can religious life be characterised in this way? Certainly many writers have answered in the negative. Both Durkheim and Pareto have argued that religious people are primarily ruled by normative beliefs or sentiments

3. It is significant that in so far as Barth adopts a Winchian position, his style of analysis counters MacIntyre's claim that Winch cannot handle the question of why people sometimes deviate from normative rules (see MacIntyre, 1967 :96, 101).

and so do not tend to play games by juggling around with their religions in order to attain various empirical (and social) ends. We shall return to this question of the relevance of the individualistic means-ends schema in our discussion of magic.

As a final point, however, it should be noted that it is in the context of religious ritual that the difference between belief and action systems is minimised. This issue can be approached by considering why the means-end, rule-governed approach has most commonly been applied in the context of explaining action rather than belief. Part of the answer is that whereas 'Explaining actions is explaining choices' (MacIntyre, 1962 : 61), choice is not so important in those belief systems that are found in primitive cultures. The conservative nature of primitive religious systems means that there is little scope for choice in the form of argument. Conceptual relations are given by the systems—and the same can be said for religious rituals. This is because they differ from those kinds of social activity where agents have to adjust their means in order to take into account contingent circumstances. Religious ritual creates its own circumstances, and so typically allows for as little choice as does religious belief. Even moral action—which logically relies on the possibility of choice—is largely a matter of simply acting in terms of one's beliefs. Thus in the context of ritual, which often takes a moral form, one of the most important ways of distinguishing between belief and action systems tends to fade away. Ritual, as will become apparent in our discussion of magic, is often best analysed in terms of rules and meanings, not rules and choices.

One of the great debates in the anthropology of religion has concerned the nature of magic. The debate is of particular interest to us because one of the main reasons why it has persisted is to be found in an explanatory limitation of the notion of rule. I shall argue that because of the limitation we cannot ever expect to gain a clear understanding of magic.

A typical instance of magic is provided by the person who sows his seeds and cultivates his crops in accordance with recognised technological methods, but who also finds it necessary to visit a dignitary who engages in ritual, apparently to ensure that the harvest is successful. Since our paradigm of understanding rule-governed activity is provided by instrumental action governed by intrinsic rationality (where means are related to ends in a 'scientifically' acceptable fashion), it is not difficult to understand the clearly technological aspect of this individual's action. One applies the logic of the situation approach, treating the act as an instance of the means-end action schema.

However, it is by no means clear how one can best interpret the associated ritual. Some anthropologists have argued that magic is an instance of misapplied technological activity (e.g. Frazer, 1890; Jarvie and Agassi, 1970). One reason why they have been persuaded that ritual can often be interpreted as a causally efficacious means of acquiring empirical ends is that such rituals are intimately associated with successful technological activities. And they have treated the rituals as error because, from their positivistic viewpoint, the ritual means are not related to the empirical ends by beliefs which are 'properly' (according to the scientific model of cause and effect) linked to empirical reality.

Other anthropologists have suggested that magic is best portrayed as the symbolic expression of social, natural and existential states of affairs. This approach can be subdivided in order to distinguish between the position adopted by Beattie (1970), where account is taken of the apparently instrumental aspect of magic, and the position adopted by Wittgenstein (1971) and Winch (1967), where the symbol-meaning style of interpretation stands in greatest contrast to the means-end approach. Thus for Wittgenstein, 'magic always rests on the idea of symbolism and of language'. Magic does things, but only in the sense of being highly expressive:

> The description (*Darstellung*) of a wish is, *eo ipso*, the description of its fulfilment.
> And magic does give representation (*Darstellung*) to a wish; it expresses a wish (: 31).

How can we decide between these different accounts of the nature of magic? I have argued elsewhere that much can be done by tracing the consequences of these positions in order to show that they lead to implausible conclusions (Heelas, 1974a). More fundamentally, however, we can perhaps settle the issue by closely examining the nature of magic as manifested in various social and cultural contexts. And this, if we follow the Wittgenstinian–Winchian view of meaning, is a matter of understanding magic by equating the meaning of the relevant notions with learning how to use them in accordance with rules.

This is where the difficulties arise. Wittgenstein suggests that religious symbols (including, it would seem, those employed in magic) do 'not rest on any *opinion*' (1971 : 30, see also : 37). Many anthropologists would agree because they have found it well-nigh impossible to elicit from informants those reasons for practising magic which one might expect to find. The situation is, in fact, a curious one. On the one hand informants will often say that they practise magic in order to attain empirical ends. This encourages the view that magic is mis-applied technological action. But on the other hand, precisely because informants cannot easily be persuaded to give detailed reasons as to why they practise magic to attain such ends (*viz.* why they apply 'odd' means to attain their goals), the activity would appear to take a sym-bolic form. In other words, because magic generally lacks 'opinions' of the cognitive and verificationist type which tends to inform techno-logical action, one is inclined to conclude that the notions involved in magic are of a highly expressive nature.

Part of the process of explaining a technological act involves show-ing how the point of the act is related to the application of the means. Thus in our seed-sowing example the nature and meaning of the act would differ if, for instance, the sower were engaged in a seed-sowing competition. If he had entered such a competition, his goal would influence his choice of means. Yet as we have seen in the case of magic it is extremely difficult to show that the apparent point of the act (i.e. attaining empirical ends) is related to the means in accordance with the trial and error strategy of technological action. Together with the fact that participants cannot generally say much about their magic, this is strong *prima facie* evidence that the rules that constitute and regulate magic differ from the verificationist-governed variety manifested in technological acts, where the participant can explain why he employs certain means to attain his goal.

We have to conclude that the nature of the rules of magic cannot be deduced from the apparent (instrumental) point of magic; we also have to conclude that since the rationality of these rules cannot readily be portrayed as the consequence of trial and error reasoning, they must basically be about the ritual use of words or acts rather than about the regulation of technological action. The rules, it appears, simply constitute and govern the identification, appropriateness and coherence of the utterances employed in magic.

Unfortunately, however, this does not say very much, for it would seem that we must somehow break into the system of magic to estab-lish the nature of these rules and the meanings which they constitute. One method is to analyse the relations between utterances used in magic and the same utterances when they are used in non-magical contexts (cf. Ramsey, 1957). Thus a crucial notion in magic would appear to be that of *cause*, for if this were not the case the problem of instrumentality would not arise. If the indigenous term for cause is X, then to understand what X means in more accessible contexts will give us at least *some* idea of its magical sense. But this does not help us very much. It is precisely because magic is (apparently) unlike those activities performed in contexts which provide relatively easy translations of such notions as cause, that we call the rituals 'magical'.

If this does not enable us to get adequate leverage on the meanings of words used in the context of magic, we might perhaps engage in intra-magic analysis of the type used by Evans-Pritchard in connection with expressions such as 'birds are twins'. We have already said enough to show that magic does not contain sufficiently clear propositional rules to make this profitable. What, then, of asking participants to talk about the meaning of their propositional rules and beliefs? Consider the lover from our own culture who is kissing a locket containing the hair of his beloved. We ask him, 'Why are you doing this and what does it mean?' Typically, he will fumble for words, perhaps replying, 'I suppose I'm not really kissing her; perhaps I'm not trying to kiss her at all. I think I'd better say I'm expressing my feelings towards her.' The ethnographer then objects, 'But surely, by kissing *her hair* you're acting as though you believe in some kind of causal efficacy linking her hair and her being.' The participant is then forced to say, 'No, that's not true, her hair is just a convenient symbol.'

The ethnographer's attempts to clarify the issues succeeds in distorting the nature of what he is trying to understand. In Wittgenstein's example, the game which can always be won by the person who makes the first move, because this person unselfconsciously applies a simple trick, ceases to be a game once this has been pointed out (quoted in Winch 1967 : 23). One of the characteristic properties of magic lies in its unselfconsciousness. As MacIntyre has pointed out, it is therefore all too easy to ask inappropriate questions, questions which lead participants to conceptualise their activities, thereby distorting them (1971 : 252). In our example, the line of questioning might well have resulted in an overemphasis on the expressive aspect of the act.

Largely because of the virtual absence of propositional rules of the type which can be established in such contexts as the Nuer's 'birds are twins', it is exceedingly difficult to determine the nature of the rules and meanings employed in magic. We are left in the position described by these lines from a popular song:

You know all the words and you sang all the notes
But you never quite learned the song she sung,
I can tell by the sadness in your eyes that you
Never quite learned the song. . . .

The full meaning of the song is not equivalent to learning how to
sing it; the full meaning rests, in fact, on grasping its point, realising
what the song is about and what it is trying to do. For if the song is
about ecstatic love then it will have a different meaning from that
where its purpose is to convey anguish.

We have already seen how the end to which technological action is
directed affects the nature of the act. In similar fashion, if one case of
magic is about 'the majesty of death' (see Wittgensteain 1971 : 30),
another about morality (as often appears to be the case with witch-
craft), and yet another about attaining empirical ends (as could be the
case in some alchemical practices), we would have to seek different types
of rules, different meanings, and then apply different styles of interpretation. Simply learning how to practise magic mechanically does not
penetrate to the nature of magic, to what it is really about. Hence
MacIntyre's quarrel with the suggestion 'that agreement in following
a rule is sufficient to guarantee making sense' (1970a : 68), and hence
Winch's observation that it is necessary for us 'to consider the relation
of a set of rules and conventions to something else' (1967 : 36).

The types of reality embedded in any one type of magic gives it its
point; what magic is about fundamentally affects the nature of its rules
and meaning. But how are we to establish what the 'something else'
might be? If we accept Winch's claim that 'Our idea of what belongs
to the realm of reality is given for us in the language that we use'
(1971 : 15), then the only way to grasp the nature of the reality which,
by being 'symbolised' in magic, gives it its meaning, is by semantic
investigation. But as we have argued, it is not easy to draw inferences
from the utterances or acts of participants to the nature of the underlying reality. The notion of rule, where it is related to the idea that
'meaning is use', does not take us as far as we would like.

The utility of the notion is further weakened by the fact that some
cases of magic involve a type of reality which engenders a view of
meaning which is not equivalent to its use. Waismann has argued that
the view of meaning as use cannot always 'explain the *whole* meaning'.
He continues:

Is [this] not indeed the case with such expressions as 'sorrow', 'homesickness', 'horror', 'foreboding', and with many feelings and moods that are indefinite and difficult to communicate accurately? We can understand these words to a certain extent, but we cannot appreciate them as fully as one who has himself experienced the feelings (1965 : 265).

Unlike MacIntyre (1970b), Malcolm (1972) and many others, Waismann (1968) is prepared to supplement the meaning-is-use view by applying a view of language as a 'bridge built by the mind to lead from consciousness to consciousness' (: 268). Thinking back to the song, simply to learn to sing it is to know the words 'only from the outside'; to know what it is about is to learn its 'inner meaning' (: 266). 'We understand a sentence just as we understand a piece of music, entirely from inside' (: 363). Much the same idea is reflected in Wittgenstein's interpretation of Frazer's account of the King of the Wood at Nemi:

. . . what strikes us in this course of events as terrible, impressive, horrible, tragic, etc., anything but trivial and insignificant, *that* is what gave birth to them. . . . Put that account of the King of the Wood at Nemi together with the phrase 'the majesty of death', and you see that they are one (1971 : 30).

The language we use might give us our idea of what belongs to the realm of reality, but the inner meaning of at least some instances of magic would appear to be derived from an existential realisation of the signified elements or underlying realities. We cannot always grasp the full nature of magic by applying the relatively formalistic and abstract rule schema. Rules are necessary conditions for meaningful discourse, but since rules only constitute meaning in so far as they regulate the use of words, can we not allow that words also have what Waismann calls 'inner meaning'?

Let me illustrate the point with an example drawn from my field-work among the Sherpas of Nepal. Their notion of 'cause' can quite readily be translated. I gave examples of the various ways we use the term (e.g. causing a car to go by mending the engine, causing someone to leave the room by being rude, etc.), and gathered from my main informant that the Sherpa word for cause has similar scope. Furthermore, just as in our own culture there is a close connection between the notions of cause, compulsion, and power (cf. Waismann, 1968 : 209), so too the Sherpas say that lama can only cause (or make) the rain fall because he has sufficient power.

We can partly grasp what this means; we can grasp that the lama's ritual involves making it rain. But I do not think that the notion of cause has the same meaning in magical and non-magical contexts. This is because the magical usage is intimately associated with one of the various (and complex) ways in which Sherpas speak of power. They describe magic itself as *natungtab*, which, roughly translated, means 'more than normal power'. So the lamas can cause (or make) the rain fall because the possess a peculiar type of power. And the nature of this power determines the meaning of 'causing it to rain'.

The meaning of the term *natungtab* is of the essence. But although we can elicit a certain amount of information about this term (by examining how the Sherpas compare it with their other notions of power), its inner meaning is exceedingly difficult to grasp. The term is unique to the context of lama magic, and this type of power is obtained via the gods. It appears that its full meaning can only be grasped by somehow experiencing what it is to be a lama engaging in magic (cf. Winch, 1971 : 88; Wittgenstein, 1971 : 30–41; Evans-Pritchard, 1956 : 322). Such a realisation is necessary, says Waismann, if one is to acquire 'the ability to describe imaginatively all the subtle implications of the word' (1968 : 266). But, as Waismann also observes, if one tries to explicate inner meanings one usually has to return to simply presenting something very akin to what one is trying to explicate. He concludes that 'in this sense every language in the end must speak for itself' (: 363). This conclusion is curiously suited to his argument that because experiences (or inner meanings) are of a private nature, 'it is doubtful how far language really bridges the chasm between soul and soul' (: 268).

Magic is left to speak for itself when we, as outsiders, have little realisation of what magic is about. If the argument is correct, magic is likely to remain a partially understood phenomenon. I am not denying that a certain amount of progress has been made. For instance, we are now much more aware of the contexts in which magic is typically employed, and much can be learned by showing that the magic of primitive societies is to be found in our own society. More fundamentally, we are learning to be less positivistic, in that we are learning to be more cautious about imposing a 'point' on magic by assuming that it involves a technological use of the term cause (see Winch, 1967 : 34–6; MacIntyre, 1971 : 252; Tambiah, 1973 : 199–203). However, as we have seen, it is one thing to argue that cases of magic might involve subtle meanings of 'cause', or even meanings which are best translated in other terms, and quite another to specify what these meanings might be.[4] For this reason, I doubt that we will ever be able to establish *conclusively*, for instance, whether instances of magic are regulated by rules which somehow involve reasoning about the empirical world, or whether they are regulated by rules whose rationale has to do with the interplay of metaphor and experience which they express or evoke.

Having dealt at some length on a limitation of the notion of rule, I do not want to leave the impression that it is without any utlity. So I shall conclude by arguing that the notion of following a rule has greater explanatory force than is usually recognised, and that it can provide the basis for a powerful semantic anthropology of religion. In the last fifteen years or so, it has become increasingly apparent that traditional, positivistically inclined anthropology has not been able to cope satisfactorily with the demanding task of offering new insights into the nature of religious phenomena. Positivism has proved to be inadequate for three main and interrelated reasons: theoretical stagnation, neglect of meaning, and neglect of intra-religious explanations (see Geertz, 1966). The rule approach can generate new 'theories', concentrate on meaning, and analyse religion 'from within'.

The main reason why the approach can usefully be adopted is that it allows us to study the religious as the religious. This can be grasped by considering Radcliffe-Brown's (1952) positivistic account of social sanction in the context of Winch's claim that 'Our idea of what belongs to the realm of reality is given for us in the language that we use. . . . The world *is* for us what is presented through those concepts' (1971 : 15). Radcliffe-Brown established a correlation between primary sanctions and social sentiments, applying a psychological theory to give the connection causal significance. Two striking aspects of his theory are that the primary sanctions are held to constitute the 'machinery of social control' and that 'What is called conscience is . . . in the widest sense the reflex in the individual of the sanctions of the society' (: 208, 205). Morality, in the form of sanctions, is grounded in mechanistic

---

4. Richards has drawn attention to the various meanings of the term 'cause', and to how difficult, yet important, it is to distinguish between these senses in anthropological enquiry (1964 : 3; see also Winch, 1967 : 34). It is also interesting to note that the Chinese word *ku* can be translated as 'cause' and 'reason'. Perhaps our philosophical debate over the distinction between explanation in terms of causes and explanation in terms of reasons would not have arisen had we spoken Chinese!

and deterministic processes. Yet as has often been pointed out, from the participant point of view and from the point of view of philosophy, the very meaning of moral life requires that agents can exercise free choice (cf. Winch, 1971 : 65).

Radcliffe-Brown is not talking about morality as it is maintained by participants. And if we agree with Winch's view of the relationship between reality and language, Radcliffe-Brown is no longer talking about morality at all. To help clarify this, we can introduce MacIntyre's argument that 'if what the agent does is to count as an example of an action at all, his action is identified fundamentally *as what it is* by the description under which he deems it to fall' (1962 : 58). To give a causal account of morality is to introduce non-participant notions (e.g. 'machinery') that contradict the essential meaning of morality, namely freedom of choice.

Now even if we admit that Radcliffe-Brown's account is scientifically acceptable, the fact remains that it is only by adopting Winch's position that morality can be adequately studied as a participant-based phenomenon. Rule-governed analysis takes us beyond causal analysis, allowing us to study the conceptual intricacy and complexity of moral life. To give one example, Radcliffe-Brown's theory of sanctions is ill-suited for examining cultural response to evil. It is not especially enlightening to be told that evil deeds bring about 'social dysphoria', which is then handled by the application of sanctions. Much more interesting issues are raised if instead one treats evil as a meaningful reality, examining the logic of cultural responses. Thus in the case of Christianity, morality can be portrayed as a complex rule-governed rationale involving, amongst other things, an all-loving God, a Saviour, forgiveness, individual responsibility, conscience, guilt, sin, and sometimes the Devil. Instead of being directed to the sociological functions of the moral apparatus, the intra-religious approach leads us to examine the rule-governed nature of cultural solutions to the existence of evil.

Although I have concentrated on Radcliffe-Brown's theory of moral sanctions, the limitations due to the positivistic relocation procedure are perhaps evident in the work of most anthropologists of religion (see Heelas, 1974a). Aside from the case of magic, we might bear in mind the semantic impoverishment which occurs if one adopts Leach's 'simply about social behaviour' view of myth, Lewis' sociological reductionist approach to spirituality (1971), and so forth. Durkheimians—and most British anthropologists of religion have adopted the general Durkheimian position—have tended to ignore many important aspects of religious life. They have felt little need to present detailed semantic analyses of the type which are addressed to such questions as, 'How is the inexpressible expressed in various religions?'. In their theoretical framework, spiritual entities are treated as symbols of empirical states of affairs, so they have no incentive to study how these entities are expressed within the participant's frame of reference. Furthermore, we simply do not possess scientific theories capable of portraying and explaining the conceptual intricacies of the devices which are used to express the inexpressible. The devices of metaphor, analogy, paradox, silence and disclosure can be examined in terms of their rationale but not in terms of scientific theories. The same applies to another set of conceptual relationships of crucial importance in many religions, namely the interplay between 'psychological' concepts, such as the notion of mind, and more strictly religious notions such as immanence (see Lienhardt, 1961; Heelas, 1974b). Finally, it is also possible to examine the various types of rule-governed balance which are struck in different religions with respect to such distinctions as immanence/transcendence, world-rejecting/world encompassing, prayer/meditation, and peace/moral worth.

The notion of rule lies at the core of semantic anthropology. It appears in connection with the idea of meaning-is-use, rationality, the regulation of moral life, the explanation of religious activities, and the rationale of religious systems. I shall close by briefly considering the last of these aspects. Lévi-Strauss has made the remark that 'There is certainly something paradoxical about the idea of a *logic* whose terms consist of odds and ends left over from psychological processes and are, like these, devoid of necessity' (1966 : 35, my emphasis). But can we hope to show that there is a necessity at work in the forms taken by religious rationales? For if religious systems can be shown to be derived from processes which are scientifically explicable, it would follow that the relations within the systems are contingent, for only logical or conceptual relations are of a necessary order.

It appears that we are in the position of having to say that a relationship between x and y religious phenomena is of a necessary order if it is understood in terms of logic or rules, but of a contingent order if it is understood in terms of a scientific theory. However, the point is that many such relations cannot be scientifically understood without altering their nature. To illustrate this, consider the hypothetical rule that when the numinous feeling-state is important, religious language will be highly elliptical, but when it is unimportant religious language will be literalistic. If this is interpreted in terms of logic, the explanation runs that the meaning of the numinous is such that it requires (or entails) that religious language take certain forms. If, on the other hand, the interpretation is scientific, a theory could maintain, for instance, that what religious people call the numinous is in fact a psychological state that makes them adopt particular forms of religious language. The nature of the relationship has been altered in that 'theological' argument, and therefore logic, has a role to play in the first account (e.g. the numinous is too holy to be spoken of directly), but not the second.

Thus, so long as we remain within the domain of intra-religious explanation, we may expect to find a degree of logical necessity operative in the constitution and regulation of patterns of religious systems, even though this necessity might disappear where theories are applied to show that the configurations are in fact determined by sociological or psychological processes. In any case, the fact that such scientific theories might be applicable need not worry the semantic anthropologist. For his ultimate task is to discern those rules, of the basic type, *If religious phenomenon A, then phenomenon B*, which logically determine the pattern found in religions. He wants to be able to trace the logical possibilities which follow from a certain religious phenomenon, or to show that a cluster of beliefs or meaningful experiences constrains the system in such a way as to 'necessitate' other phenomena.

I have argued that the rationale of religious symbol systems is largely determined by principles of rationality and by propositional rules, these being the conceptual implications of basic assertions of the type we outlined in connection with Nuer religion. Basic propositional rules regulate what goes with what in the sense of rendering only certain forms of conceptual relationships appropriate. They also, so to speak, identify beliefs and actions as having particular forms of symbolic meaning. The coherence of the system is also regulated by rules of rationality or logic which are separate from propositional rules but which work in close conjunction with them. In other words, the propositional rules do not in themselves state the manner in which their implications are to be construed. They do not state what type of rationality is to be applied to their implications. By way of illustration let us imagine an alchemical text which informs us that immortality can be attained by changing base metal into gold. This rule could be followed in at least two ways. It could be taken to imply that one should build complicated retorts, or it could be taken to imply that one should purify one's mind. This issue can only be settled by establishing the point of the rule. If the point is to accumulate wealth, then its implications have to be construed in terms of intrinsic rationality involving trial and error and the construction of workable apparatus, whereas if the point is to be taken metaphorically then its implications have to be derived from the symbolic rationality.[5] Thus, the point of the alchemical text functions to impose rationality on the basic rule, this rationality selecting and then directing one of the sets of implications inherent in the basic rule.

There is much more to be said about the rules which determine the rationales and hence configurations found in religious systems. It is clear, for example, that the anthropology of religion would make great strides if it were able to establish more rules of the type discerned by Nadel when he observed that 'you may have a God of Justice and Mercy, naïvely conceived, and devils or witches in the background; or you may have an Idle God, remotely in the background, but at least devils or witches to grapple with' (1954 : 204).[6] Symbolic systems are neither entirely arbitrary nor fully determined by sociological processes. And their symbolic character means that they are not in any important sense regulated by intrinsic rationality. Hence the possibility of formulating rules of cross-cultural scope. We may conclude that the semantic anthropology of religion will come of age when it has established a number of principles or rules operative in those aspects of religion which lie beyond the compass of positivistic enquiry.

5. I have discussed the rules of rationality in the context of their point or function. Thus attaining empirical ends encourages the logic of trial and error, while expressing the inexpressible encourages the use and logic of models and qualifiers (see Ramsey, 1957). The style of argument concerning the enforcement of a schema of conduct is very different from that concerning the nature of the world (see Richards, 1964). However, some have suggested an alternative approach in which rules are considered in the context of the psychology of the primitive mind (see Hallpike, 1975).

6. Other useful examples of similar rules are to be found in Winch's discussion of what he calls 'limiting notions' (1967 : 38), his argument that social life necessarily involves the virtues of truthfulness (1972 : 50–72), and in Smart's portrayal of a 'religious logic' (1973). Smart's *The Science of Religion and the Sociology of Knowledge* (1973) contains, in my opinion, the best account of what I have portrayed as the semantic approach. The work is, however, somewhat marred by rather loose usage of such terms as 'theory', and as a result he obscures the distinction presented in the first section of this paper.

The Inherent Rules
of Violence
ROBIN FOX

In this paper I want to ask something about the very nature of social rules as exemplified in fighting, about what might be called the 'rules of violence'. Unfortunately, once we begin to talk about violence and aggression we get into all sorts of semantic problems. But I will not be concerned here with those. Instead I will focus on fighting, as in punch-ups, when people actually engage in physical combat with each other. We don't have any definitional problems here; we all know what fighting is. Thinking about fighting and having, in the course of my own field work, had to watch and extricate myself from, and generally be concerned with, fighting, I consider that it raises certain problems about the very nature of social rules which are germane to anthropological debate. So I shall begin with a few remarks on the issue of rules and behaviour in order to show why I am interested in fighting in this respect.

There seem to be two issues that one can pin down: one is the anthropological-sociological position that rules as such represent 'culture' as opposed to 'nature'. You get this notion in all kinds of guises. Rules are seen as—to use Lévi-Strauss' (1969) expression—an 'intrusion into nature'; they are an aspect of the super-organic, the non-genetic heritage of men. Basically, the fact that we order our lives according to rules is what divides us from nature. Nature, we are told, may have regularities but it does not have rules. So human behaviour is primarily different from animal behaviour because it is rule-governed. Now in a sense this is obviously true if one thinks of rules in the sense of edicts or laws, because animals don't have language

and self-consciousness and they don't make laws. This is therefore
almost a trivial sort of truth. It is a characteristic of this particular
species, *Homo sapiens*, that one aspect of its species-specific behaviour,
if you like, is that it makes rules. But then, I think, we need to ask,
what is the significance of this as the basis of a nature-culture distinction? Lévi-Strauss, for example, takes incest. Animals have incest, we
have rules against incest, and this he makes the great dividing line
between nature and culture. Actually, when we look at animals, they
have about as much incest as we do, by and large, if we look at what we
do as opposed to what we *say* we do. If you simply compare human
behaviour with animal behaviour you find that in nearly all species of
animals there are quite elaborate mechanisms preventing incestuous
inbreeding, or at least two-thirds of it. They will exclude mother and
daughter, and brother and sister, and leave in father and daughter, or
something to that effect. But most of the 'weight' of inbreeding, as it
were, gets taken out by some mechanism or another. In our case it is
much the same; we remove the bulk of incest but we leave in some. So
the question then becomes, what is the significance of these rules if, as
far as actual behaviour is concerned, there is no firm distinction
between animals and man?

What are these rules doing, these incestuous rules? Are they really
intrusions into nature, are they really attempts, as Lévi-Strauss suggests,
to say 'No' to Nature, or are they simply, as I think they are in many
cases, labellings of natural tendencies? That is, do we simply put into
words and formulate into rules things that we would do anyway in the
absence of language or self-consciousness. I am not saying they are or
they are not, I am just saying that it seems to me to be an open question
as to whether or not in many cases rules are simply labellings of
natural tendencies and therefore not in any sense anti-nature or an
intrusion into nature. The sort of work I've been doing on kinship
systems comes to a similar conclusion (Fox, 1967). Roughly speaking, I
think we can carefully put together all kinds of evidence which
suggests, again, that in the absence of language and self-consciousness,
we as a species would probably have kinship systems that were recognisable in terms of very regular patterns of discriminatory behaviour
towards kin. That is, we would probably have lineages and alliances
and all the things that we find in human kinship systems. What we
do with human kinship systems is to label all these things. Once you
label them you then get a feedback effect and you begin to play games
with the labels and the whole symbolism of kinship systems emerges.

A great deal of the time what we are doing is labelling 'natural' tendencies, not in any sense intruding into nature. I think that Lévi-Strauss has this mistaken notion in that he confuses rules with order: we have rules, animals do not, therefore animal life is unordered. Animals mate promiscuously and are incestuous, we mate selectively and are not incestuous, and that's because of rules. Well, the answer is that animal life is not so chaotic; it's incredibly ordered, and if you're going to make that kind of mistake you are back to the old 'law of nature' and 'law as edict' confusion again. Certainly, coming from a Frenchman, this idea that human mating is not promiscuous and disordered is rather curious!

I raise these various problems very briefly in order to ask, if you like, 'what price rules?' Now, one can find various cases in which it's fairly clear that rules *are* intrusive, that is they do say 'No' to nature, and that they do somehow formulate a kind of behaviour that is wholly peculiar to man. I think we could probably winkle out some systems of that kind. But a lot of the time I think that rules are what I call simply labelling devices for things that would happen anyway.

This takes me on to the second and related question. This is the question which, I suppose, lies behind all anthropology and social psychology, and that is the question of social order—what I prefer here to phrase as the 'Hobbes-versus-Aristotle' issue. For Hobbes (1642), the state of nature is a 'war of all against all'. We are told that life is 'poor, nasty, brutish and short', so that in order to attain a state of culture, or a state of civil society if you like, you have to have a social contract, which is the first rule. Basically, a social contract involves the instigation of rules in order to bring order to a previously disordered state of nature, in which every man's hand is turned against that of every other man. I think Hume (1739) was the first critic, in this sense the first really acute social psychologist to point out that most of human behaviour is of course not ordered by explicit rules, contracts, agreements or the like, but, as he put it, is ordered by 'conventions'. He gives the example of two oarsmen in a boat who have no specific contract or agreement as to how they will row, but who nevertheless end up rowing perfectly in time and pulling the boat. This is his model for most social conventions. We all end up somehow pulling the boat in the same direction without ever having agreed that we will do it in any particular way. Again, at the bottom of this whole contract theory is the notion that rules order nature; if you did not have rules, agreements, conventions or whatever, you would have disorder.

This Hobbesian notion appears to have stuck with us. It is basic to most of the empiricists' and environmentalists' views that, in the absence of rules that are established through material interest, there would be disorder. Against this there is the Aristotelian tradition, which says that man is *by nature* a social animal (I think it's Tiger who keep pointing out how curious it is that whenever this gets quoted people leave out 'by nature'). This tradition holds that society precedes culture, that society is part of nature and that it is perfectly natural for men to live in a rule-governed situation. In so doing they are not somehow imposing themselves on nature, they are not making a radical change. They are *expressing* their nature. They are social animals and they will therefore live in a civil state. You get this tradition warring rather weakly against the Hobbesian tradition in the nineteenth century, in people like Espinas, who was Durkheim's teacher but whose book, *Des Sociétés Animales* (1877) was, as far as I know, never translated into English. In Bradley (1876) we find the first social psychologist to anticipate theories of status and role. And of course in Darwin (1871) we find implicit this same notion which Bradley advances, namely the idea that rules are an inherent part of the nature of the creature, and not something imposed upon the nature of the creature. Bergson (1935) had this same idea in his notion of the evolution of the two kinds of life processes, intelligence and instinct. He pointed out how intelligent animals have to re-create out of their intelligence almost quasi-instinctual societies, because you cannot stop and think about every move. Here he is back to Hume's conventions again: you need to have a whole set of hidden understandings, according to which everybody will work, and you end up behaving as though you were driven by instincts, even though in fact you are not. This Hobbes-versus-Aristotle issue, this question of social order, is linked, I think, with the anthropological-sociological notion of rules as an imposition on nature. Lévi-Strauss takes incest as his perfect example of the institution of a rule. The incest taboo, he thinks, is a perfect example because it partakes of both nature and culture. It is at the fulcrum between nature and culture, it is universal, it occurs everywhere. Hence, he suggests, it is part of nature, but is it also rule-governed and hence part of culture, so it is *the rule*, the essential rule that gets all culture going. But as I said before, I think he is wrong here, because we would have incest avoidance even if we did not have taboos and rules.

Now I want to look at the same issue as regards fighting. If you take fighting you can assume that, as in the promiscuous incestuous state that Lévi-Strauss and no doubt Hobbes have imagined to be the natural state of man, you would have disordered Hobbesian mayhem. You have it in promiscuous incestuous mating, you have it in fighting— a very similar thing. When you are down to the fisticuffs and the adrenalin is surging through the body, and all those hormonal changes are occurring, and the blood is up and so on, you would imagine that you had somehow returned to a pre-cultural level. Here you somehow abandon the world of rules, the world of culture, the world of order, of reason, of categories, of cognition, of self-consciousness—all those wonderful things that make us men. When we begin a punch-up, we are somehow back to the 'natural' animal state. However, the more closely I look at fighting, from the individual pub brawl up to some of the most intricate organised warfare the more obvious it becomes that fighting is heavily rule-governed; it is rule-governed in the same way that language is rule-governed, where none of us are aware of the rules of language but where nevertheless we speak according to them. In other words, it is very rare to find fighting that is random, disorderly, totally unstructured. Therefore what I'm asking about fighting is, is there something going on here that is the same as occurs in incest or kinship or anything else, namely that there are certain *inherent* rules of violence? Is there something 'inherent' about the very structuring of fighting, and if so, then what is it? Furthermore, are many of the rules— the explicit rules, the Queensberry rules, the Geneva Conventions, the elaborate rules that we weave around fighting—attempts at social contracts, attempts to impose rules on this mayhem of natural blood-letting, or are they labelling devices? Are they merely elaborate cultural expressions of what would happen even in the absence of explicit rules, consciousness and so forth?

Well, that is my idea and there is really not much more to say except to describe some aspects of fighting as I have observed it on Tory Island. The name Tory is derived from the Gaelic word for 'robber' or 'brigand' which was the basis of the insult that was thrown by the Whigs at the Kings' Party in the eighteenth century. People ask me if it is an island for retired Conservative MPs, but it isn't. It's a small island, three miles long, widest a mile wide, with nearly 300 people living on it. They are all Gaelic speakers, all Roman Catholics and living a life that is relatively removed from what goes on on the Mainland. The islanders kicked the landlord's bailiff out in 1861, after which nobody really gained much control over them. A gunboat was sent to try to collect their rents and rates but the gunboat sank and fifty men were killed. The Admiralty said it was a navigational error, but the islanders all know that it was the king in fact who turned the cursing stones on the boat and sank it. There is no point in my going into a long description of the island, except to say that it's nine miles off the shore, very remote and very difficult to get to. It's one of the last really archaic bits of Celtic twilight left to us. So you can imagine this little island, with its tiny harbour, its cluster of houses and, of course, a church.

It would be wrong to give the impression that Tory Islanders spend most of their time fighting. But on those infrequent occasions when fights do occur, they become matters of intense interest, and the cleavages and tensions of the whole community are brought resoundingly to the surface.

I will leave aside the question of why the Irish have a reputation for bellicosity, as well as the question of why they are so bellicose. Certainly communities differ, and so may national characters, in the amount of violence they tolerate or encourage. There are several ways they can handle violence. They can forbid it altogether and punish those who resort to it, which is really a matter of reserving 'legitimate' violence for the governors of the community or the state. They can bring up their children to avoid violence except as a last resort. Or they can allow violence only under certain restricted conditions—such as in sports, or in 'legal' manhunts. But there is no one way of dealing with the potentially disruptive effects of violence. It is sometimes said that there are communities that are totally nonviolent, but this can easily be refuted. Pueblo Indians, Eskimos, Bushmen, have all been cited as examples of nonviolent people, and all turn out to have high rates of personal violence. The Bushmen of the Kalahari Desert, it turns out, have a higher homicide rate than Chicago! A book was written about them called *The Harmless People*, which only goes to show that while anthropologists might be nice folk who like to think well of their fellow men, they can be poor guides to reality.

Violence can be channelled, suppressed, repressed and variously kept in corners, where it can fester largely unobserved by those not looking for it or not wanting to see it. But it is a rare community of human beings that does not have its quota of violent activity. It is interesting not to try to explain this away somehow but to see how it is handled. Another fact must be faced: violence is pleasurable. We have to face up to the fact that violence generates tremendous excitement, either in participation or in observation, and this seems to be a

universal and deep-seated facet of our behaviour, so that it's very easy
to teach us to enjoy violence. In other words, we may not by nature be
aggressive killers, but it is terribly easy to turn us into them. It is in
fact so easy that it suggests that the animal must be rather ready to
learn this pattern of behaviour in the same way as it is ready to learn
language.

I do not think that Tory men are 'by nature' more violent than other
men. In most of their dealings they are gentle and considerate. But they
have a threshold of anger and, once it is reached, they are quick to
respond with aggressive acts—always, however, in defence of what they
perceive as their legitimate interests. The tensions that can occur on a
densely populated little island with few resources are without number.
There is no authority other than the priest—and how much influence he
has is open to question.[1]

When alcohol is brought to the island, as it from time to time, and
rapidly consumed, there is a consequent lowering of inhibitions.
Quarrels at the verbal level are rare, and antagonists will usually just
avoid each other. A visitor to the island will be surprised when,
suddenly, a fight starts for seemingly no reason and with few prelimi-
naries. At first sight, it seems to be an unstructured scuffle. But this is
the main point I want to make about Tory fights: they are never
unstructured. This may seem strange, for it appears that fighting is
something below the level of culture and rules; that it takes men back
to something primeval, to a state of nature that is red in tooth and
claw. Perhaps. But equally primeval is the principle of ritualisation, and
I think that this is the clue to the islanders' ability to manage their
aggression. The principle of ritualisation can be stated in a general
form: in any community of animals there usually exist forms of
combat that allow antagonists to settle their differences with violent
exertion and yet with a minimum of serious damage. Sometimes the
exertion itself can become ritualised—as when an exchange of shots at a
distance in a duel of the drawing of blood in a fencing match satisfies
the honour of the antagonists. And honour is very important on the

---

1. Throughout the nineteenth century there was no priest on the island.
Occasionally, however, a visiting friar would go out to the island as a 'penance'.
When there was no priest, they would conduct marriage services by lighting fires
on the island and the mainland. The priest would stand on the mainland; as he
read one part of the service he would cover the fire, and the people on the island
would make the appropriate response. They would then cover their fire, and so it
went on.

island. The ideal outcome of an agonistic encounter is one in which the parties feel that honour has been satisfied.

In this respect the Irish attitude is quite Mediterranean. What is usually considered to be at stake when one man challenges another is honour or reputation or pride. (The whole thing is a peculiarly male affair. Women fight, but not over honour; their fighting is fierce and destructive, and almost inevitably ends in serious hurt to one of the partners. There may be a moral in this.) When a man makes a challenge he puts his pride on the line. He cannot back down without suffering a wounding hurt to his pride and a loss of reputation. It is an old story, perhaps older than history. It seems to tap something deep in men, something to do with the old interplay of dominance and virility that we see so effectively at work in nature. It is the stuff of literature, the story line of many movies. It is something the sociologically unsophisticated respond to with immediate empathy and excitement. But then the sociologist has been defined—along with the psychologist—as the man who goes to the strip-tease show to watch the audience. The obvious is the last thing he tends to see.

How is this universal theme treated on Tory? I have recorded details of some thirty fights on the island, and four off the island involving Tory men. I have details of fights from other parts of Ireland and between Irishmen in London. While they have some things in common with the Tory pattern, there are differences. On Tory there is rarely an obvious cause for a fight. The principals are usually traditional antagonists in that often they have inherited the antagonism. The fight may go back to someone's grandfather—no one knows why these two particular people fight, and they may not be very clear about it themselves. Sometimes there is a rambling story about some insult or piece of chicanery in the distant past. But for the most part no one cares. 'He's doing it to show he's a man,' they'll say. Sometimes, however, there *is* a recognisable cause—a dispute over a girl-friend, usually, or a wife or a sister, and for the usual reasons.

Here is a fight sequence. The setting is the parish hall late at night where a dance is being held. The band is playing traditional Irish dances. The old ladies on the benches along the walls look on and tap their feet. The young people are dancing a reel and getting very excited. Then the young men go to one end of the hall, near the door, where some of the older men have gathered to watch (This segregation of the sexes is important. It occurs in church, in dancing and, as we shall see, it occurs in fighting). In the ensuing lull, some of the men slip out to get bottles of Guinness, which they drink outside in the dark because after all it is illegal and the priest wouldn't like it. The priest is at the dance. He usually comes to watch for a while and, as his singing voice is much admired, is often asked to give a song. He once made an attempt to stop the dances from going on all night. He said it was bad for the children and told the hall committee to stop the dances at one o'clock at the latest. They said the people would not stand for it, that it 'was against the custom of the island'. Several lads got drunk and went and threw bottles at the priest's house. Next day they apologised and cleared up the mess. After that, the priest just left the dances at midnight and said nothing. The point of this is that there is no external authority here to interpose itself if a fight starts and the priest simply takes no notice of it.

This night, however, he did not go home at the accustomed time. There was a noise outside the hall during the lull. Shouting, curses. People rushed through the narrow door to see what was happening. A door off the stage at the other end of the hall was opened and people poured out, knocking over instruments in the rush. But it was all over by the time they got there. Old Paddy had been shouting imprecations at Wee Johnny. But Paddy had come into the hall before Wee Johnny could do anything but shout back. The crowd drifted back inside and the band struck up again. Paddy sat at the side, muttering. Suddenly, as the dance was about over, he jumped up on the stage and started to shout and kick the big drum. Several people tried to restrain him. He yelled that he would surely do some killing before the night was out. They tried to calm him but he pushed his way outside again. Wee Johnny was out there drinking with his cronies and as the doors opened a flood of light from both ends of the hall hit the dark roadway. Paddy, swinging wildly at Wee Johnny, caught him by surprise and grazed his mouth. As both men were more than a little drunk, it is unlikely that either of them could have focused well enough on the other to make an accurate hit; but Paddy's glancing blow enraged Johnny, who roared and made for his assailant. He was grabbed and held back by several hands. By now both men were rather dazed. For a while they just looked at one another—each firmly held by his supporters—and presently they began shouting insults again. Over and over Paddy repeated—my translation for the Gaelic is very rough—You don't need to hold me, I wouldn't dirty my hands with him'. Johnny replied that Paddy's hand were so dirty to start with they couldn't get any worse.

The priest came out and told everyone to go home. No one listened and soon, still protesting, he was brushed aside. The hall had emptied and most of the old ladies were now lining the roadside. At one end was Johnny's party—all men—milling about and arguing with him. At the other end was Paddy's group. Scattered between them were various groups of men not attached to either party; all around milled little boys imitating their elders, cursing, bluffing, swaggering, threatening. It was particularly fascinating to see how the children learned the whole sequence of behaviour. Anything that the men did, they would imitate, shouting the same things, strutting and swaggering. Most of the little girls stood some way off with their mothers, who had banded together to deplore the episode—quietly. So we have an arena here, the two groups of men with the principals, as it were, holding them on either side of rather amorphous groups of other men not principally attached to either group. Old ladies on either side of the road were watching, and the mothers and daughters were standing, while the little boys were running all around mimicking. The noise from Paddy's group was getting louder. Paddy was setting off down the road. The bastard, he was shouting, was going to get it this time. He'd been asking for it long enough. Several of the men on the way tried to reason with him until the main body of his supporters caught up with him and began restraining him again. They were close to Johnny's group now—about three or four yards away. Johnny moved forward and was restrained again by his men. 'Hold me back or I'll kill him for sure!' Johnny shouted again and again. The two crowds came close and even intermingled, and some minor scuffling went on. Two of Johnny's supporters began to argue and immediately attention passed to them. This seemed to annoy the principals, who began shouting again, louder now, and clawing their way through the mob to get at each other. They were pulled back, dusted down, showered with non-stop advice, and implored to cool down and go home.

Once the antagonists were separated, some of the non-partisan older men moved about between the two, waving pipes and either talking quietly or shouting (this is another instance of the old Irish principle of the intermediary. You get it when they're selling cows, arranging marriages, or almost anything else).

There was a lull in the movement during which both principals again came forward yelling at each other. The insults rose in pitch and complexity until Johnny, provoked beyond words, tore off his coat and threw it on the ground. Now this is a serious matter on Tory.

'I'll take off me coat'—this is an invitation to a real fight. As long as the coat stays on, serious fighting is not intended. But even the act of peeling back the sleeves is a drastic escalation.[2]

The coat was immediately retrieved by his group and desperate attempts were made to get it back on him again. At this point, a newcomer could have been forgiven for thinking the fight was between Johnny and those who had his coat, for he was inflicting more damage on them than he would ever get to inflict on Paddy. The coat stayed off. Now Paddy began to disrobe.

By that time everyone was sobering up, and the dash and fury of the early part of the fight were over. There was a last flurry; again the principals were pulled back; and now someone was bringing Wee Johnny's weeping mother forward; the crowd parted for the old lady. With prayers and admonitions she pleaded with Wee Johnny to come home and not disgrace her like this in front of her friends and neighbours. Saints were liberally invoked and the Blessed Virgin implored often. People hung their heads. Johnny, looking dazed, told her to quiet herself—she didn't—and hurled himself at Paddy and his group: 'I'd have had yer blood if me mother hadn't come. Ye can thank her that you're not in pieces on the road, ye scum.' Paddy spat and said nothing, and Johnny and a few of his crowd went off to his house, turning occasionally to shout back something indistinct. 'Well,' said one of the old men turning to me with a chuckle, 'and wasn't that the the great fight, for sure?' 'Right enough,' I said.

The Great Fight was the subject of discussion for days afterwards. The priest said that he would ban dances if this kind of thing ever happened again, but he was told that the hall was built by Tory men and that they would settle their affairs in their own way, according to 'the custom of the island'. The details of the fight were discussed endlessly, and various positions were taken according to how one was related to the combatants. Either Johnny was justified and Paddy a troublemaker or vice versa, or they were both troublemakers. But the excitement and interest, despite the clucking and disapproval in some quarters, was very real. When either of the principals walked through the village, everyone stopped to look respectfully. Each of them had a little more swagger than before, talked a little more aggressively; each

2. I was reading a book by Conor Cruise O'Brien (1957) on Parnell recently. He was quoting letters to the Irish Press during the Parnell scandal in which people were offering to take off their coats for Parnell, so this is obviously a pan-Irish thing, but in the fight context it becomes very important.

had shown that he was a man; each had been the centre of attention. 'A man when he has the great anger on him is a wonderful thing, is he not?' I was asked. 'He was surely,' I said, 'but weren't people disturbed by this kind of thing?' 'A nine-day wonder,' I was told; 'it never comes to anything, anyway.' The women were particularly sceptical, passing many a sharp comment about men who were quick enough to fight but ran at the sight of hard work. And one young woman laughed, 'Oh, those lads—always heroes when there's a crowd'.

The significance of this remark, and of the whole episode, was brought home to me by an extraordinary occurrence a few days later. I was up on the hillside outside the town taking photographs when I saw Johnny walking down the road alone. From the opposite direction came Paddy, also alone. Waiting for the clash, I wondered how neutral I could be, and whether I should intervene or, more likely, run for help. But Paddy passed on one side of the road, looking out to sea, and Johnny on the other, looking at the hills. Neither acknowledged my presence or the other's and each went his own way without a word.

This was my first fight and I had no reason to think that it was anything but a random affair. But some fifteen fights later, I was beginning to get bored with the predictability of the performance. There was always this stereotyped sequence of events, the insults, the rushes. There were certain conditions under which a fight would start. There had to be enough close kin of each principal on the one hand and enough related to both on the other. The close kin of each were the 'holders-back', whilst the kin of both were the 'negotiators'. This was something I learned after photographing, getting to know everybody who was in the fighting, and watching their various roles. The more closely you were related to the principal, the more you were obliged to 'hold him'; and the more distantly related—if you were related to both—the more you were obliged to try to stop the fight by negotiating. Always the 'hold me back or I'll kill him' pattern predominated; often to the extent that even when the supporters had become bored, the antagonist would go around begging to be held back.[3] The characteristic removal of the coats, the attempts to calm the men down, the pushing and scuffling, all fell into a predictable pattern. And when

3. In the account of his pilgrimage to Medina and Mecca, Sir Richard Burton (1855) describes a similar fight in which a fellow pilgrim started a quarrel with the master of a café. 'The two worthies, after a brief bandying of bad words, seized each other's throats leisurely, so as to give the spectators time and encouragement to interfere' (:216).

she was available, the mother of one of the parties was paraded, with her lines well rehearsed (or so it seemed), to bring the fight to an end. If it was not a mother, a sister might be brought on, or else a crowd of female relatives. (Again one is reminded, I suppose, of the monkeys who when they are being pursued by another male monkey will pick up an infant and hold it, and this 'cuts off' the male monkey's attack.)

The participation was always intense, as though this were the first time a fight had occurred, and after each fight the same discussions would rage. But after a while they took on for me, the punch-drunk anthropologist, the air of a ritual ballet; it was all choreographed, seemingly rehearsed, stereotyped. The language was always the same. The insults that at first had seemed so rich in their inventiveness turned up again. It began to dawn on this over-trained anthropologist that it was not mayhem and chaos, but ritual in the simplest sense. It was entirely rule-governed, even though no one could have told me what the rules were. If you sit down and ask people, 'Will you explain to me how a fight goes, what happens?', it's simply regarded as an absurd question: 'Sure you have a fight, anybody gets in there and fights, and everybody fights to hit everybody else.' The idea that there was any sequence to this, that it had in any sense a set of conventions, was quite foreign to them. Yet it was entirely rule-governed—in the same way that language is rule-governed, although only grammarians know what the rules are. And in the same way that we know when the rules are broken even if we don't know what they are, so we all knew (and deplored the fact) when the rules of the fight game were broken, as they sometimes were. For example, it was unthinkable for a group of men to set on a lone antagonist who had no kin with him, or for two lone men on a road to start a fight with no audience around. When these things did happen, there was universal condemnation. A 'proper fight' was a different matter. Two men with a quarrel—never mind what—had stood up to each other and had it out. They had shown that they were men and were willing to fight, but the situation was so structured that they seldom got hurt.

Nobody ever got more than a bloody nose out of it. No matter. Honour was salvaged by the mother's intervention; a man could not refuse a mother's prayerful pleas and obviously his opponent could not hit the old lady. Failing this, exhaustion and the pressure of kin would make each give way. But if a man actually fled, or flinched from the ordeal in any way, he lost face. Sometimes, if there were few people around, the antagonists might actually come to blows. But if the fight were managed properly, everything would eventually come out even—although each side would declare itself the winner and claim that it was the other side that had backed down, run away, or called for help. Outside the community, fights are a different matter. The fights involving Tory men that I have witnessed in Glasgow or London have been very nasty: broken bottles, boots, and gore. After one such episode, an islander ended up in the hospital with nine stitches in his scalp. But then that was in a Glasgow dance-hall. Only the police there were neutral; that is, they hit everybody just as hard, without regard to national or local origins.

I am reminded of ritual fights—or as the ethologists call them, 'agnostic encounters'—of animals. It seems that men, including Tory men, try to ritualise combat between members of the same community, much as animals do. As Lorenz has pointed out, many animals that are equipped to kill have powerful inhibitions against killing their own kind. Very often combats are reduced to exhausting wrestling or butting matches, or even to simple displays of threat and counter-threat. The stags who compete for harems at rutting time lock antlers and wrestle. Stallions, playing the same game, nip each other on the neck, instead of slashing each other with their hoofs. Some animals, like the fiddler crab with his great, exaggerated right claw or the marine iguana with his horny crest, have evolved special organs for this purpose. Man has not evolved special organs. Instead he has that remarkable organ, culture, to do this ritual work for him. Perhaps this is an example of culture building on nature, rather than as is usually assumed, running counter to it. As I said earlier, one could regard fighting as a relapse to the precultural, the pre-rule, state of nature. But nature has its way of coping with fighting among conspecifics: the fighting is ritualised so that status competition can take place without anyone getting too badly hurt (although with animals, as with humans, it doesn't always work). It might well be, then, that culturally patterned, ritualised fighting is something 'in our nature'; that men, left to themselves, will, within and even between the small communities that are their natural environment, manage to come up with elaborate bluff and threat displays that satisfy pride while doing a minimum of damage. After all, the elaborate single combat of the Greeks and Trojans cut down the killing considerably.

However, I do not want us to run away with the idea of ritualisation. It isn't all quite as simple as it has been made to be. Ritualisation is, after all, only one aspect of real conflict; fights and killings amongst conspecifics do commonly occur in nature. Schaller has that lovely phrase where he says that when one lion strays on to the territory of another lion pride, the only ritualisation available to it is to run like hell, otherwise it will be torn to pieces. It is all a matter of degree, and it seems to me that ritualisation tends to work once it is clear within the community that violence does not work, or where violence fixes the order of things anyway. In other words, if two animals find that they are so evenly matched that it would have been a fight to the death if they really tried to decide it, then they will ritualise the process between them. It would become a matter of threat, bluff and so on.

I'm reminded here of another curious institution in the west of Ireland known as the 'pub-fighter'. Very often the pub-fighter will be pointed out to you if you go into one of the bars. He has a special stool at the end of the bar which you are not to take. You see it as you come in. And the pub-fighter sits at the end with his back to the wall looking out, with his pint of stout in his left hand, and his right hand ready. I have never ever seen a pub-fighter fight, nor have I met anybody who has actually seen a pub-fighter fight. There are stories of his past fights, but that is all in the mythological past, in the time of the previous pub owner, when he beat up six men while still drinking. The pub-fighter is of course incredibly deferred to; no one would dream of starting a fight with the pub-fighter. He is treated with awe, as 'the Pub-Fighter'. So this is the kind of situation where the ritualisation has been carried to its extreme. What I am really getting at here, I suppose, is that there is a tendency to ritualise in any sort of 'steady state' situation, in any situation where animals or men have to live together as a group and where the group has to live with its neighbours. The group does not necessarily forgo violence. On the contrary, it may engage in a great deal of fighting, so that we find again this curious paradox, that there are societies in which the whole way of life is geared to fighting and violence of one sort of another, and yet there is order. They don't wipe each other out; there isn't a terrible breakdown of the social system and there aren't any of the terrible consequences one might expect entertaining a Hobbesian view of it all.

What I've described here is, I think, something that's interesting because there are no *explicit* rules. If two Tory men have a quarrel they don't go and appeal to the duelling master. What happens seems to be spontaneous. There are no written sets of rules and yet it falls into this pattern of fighting which everybody enjoys thoroughly, and through which the men can make their point without effecting too much damage. That is at one level. The next level up, I suppose, is where you do get fights between communities which are so highly ritualised that it's almost as though the business of preparing for the fight and celebrating the victory or mourning the loss is an end in itself, because the fight amounts to very little at all. I am thinking of the so-called warfare between Plains' Indians, and of the fights between villages in New Guinea. The film, *Dead Birds*, shows the fighting between villages in New Guinea, where they actually prepare the battleground by levelling the ground and engaging in other elaborate preparations.[4] When someone from a village has been ambushed and either wounded or killed, or sorcery has been practised by another village, they set out to stage a fight. Prior to the fight, all the men dress up in fantastic rigs of headgear, bones through their noses, penis sheaths, and then, carrying elaborate spears, they all meet on the battleground. There's a great deal of throwing of spears, but the spears are very big and it's very difficult to throw them accurately over a long distance, so you get fairly close, throw the spear and the young blood has to come out and dodge the spear as it comes towards him; and that's the big thing. He dodges the spear and sooner or later somebody gets hit, and as soon as somebody is hit (usually just wounded), the fight is over and everybody goes back. There is a terrific feast among the victors, and condolence and the mourning among the vanquished, and then they prepare for the next one. The whole male culture here is really devoted to fighting. They have this elaborate war-cult, much the same as with the Plains Indians.

One imagines from all the movies that Plains' Indians were for ever engaged in scalp-taking and battles. This was not the case. Most of the fighting that took place was hit-and-run, sneaky stuff in which the aim was to catch an enemy horse or to count coup on an enemy—a perfect example of ritualisation taken to the absurd. The young brave would ride towards the other group of warriors, who would fire arrows at him; he would dodge in, touch one of the enemies, and ride back; and that was the highest honour he could possibly achieve. Within both of these communities fighting between antagonists would again be highly ritualised: the fighting would be with clubs or sticks, so that damage could be inflicted without too great a likelihood of any killing.

We can also look at what happens when there is bound to be killing. Again, in a steady state relationship, there is a tendency to ritualise combat almost out of recognition. It is true even of huge combats that

4. See *The Gardens of War* (1974) by Gardner and Heider.

took place. For example, in the Mogul Wars in India, you would get as many as two hundred thousand combatants, with sixty elephants on each side and cavalry and bands and kettle-drums and the whole panoply of war. Yet it was only when things really went badly wrong that very many people got killed. You had to have two princes of equal status before you could have a war. If the other side couldn't produce a prince of equal status to yours, you wouldn't fight, the excuse being that you couldn't surrender; if your prince was defeated you could only surrender to someone of equal rank. So the two princes had to be present and since it seems that on most of these occasions the two princes had not the slightest intention of getting killed, when the battle started very quickly one of them would turn round and bolt, and of course if the prince wasn't on the battlefield the whole thing would collapse and everybody would run off home and the other side would declare itself the winner. Now people would of course get killed. You can't have two hundred thousand combatants and all these horses and arrows and guns without somebody getting killed. I think on one occasion they reckoned fifteen hundred people were killed, still a very small proportion of the mayhem that could have occurred.

Again one is reminded of medieval warfare and that great reformer, Joan of Arc, who quite spoilt the whole thing. If you remember Shaw's *St. Joan* at any rate, you recall that she explains to the French generals why they are not winning the wars and expects them to be grateful for this information, instead of which they hand her over to be burned, because she was going to spoil all the fun. She explains that they were not fighting their wars to win, but that they were fighting their enemies to knock them off their horses and take them for ransom; to which the French General replied that that was what wars were about. War was not about killing all those peasants—one could do that any time—war was about knights. The lances that they used were ridiculous. As people who set up tournaments and try to use them know, it was terribly difficult to manoeuvre a lance, to do anything but simply knock someone off his horse. It was terribly hard to do any damage to somebody protected by a ton of armour around him, and of course when he fell he could not move and so was easily captured. The whole thing was almost absurdly designed to this end. As soon as people began to take war really seriously, they had to abandon all that armour and those lances so that they could be mobile and actually kill people.

Even in eighteenth-century warfare there was this tendency to ritualise. Was it not at Malplaquet that the French General strolled over to the English side and said, 'Tirez le premier, Monsieur l'Anglais', and then strolled back again? So the English accepted the offer, fired first and decimated his army. Wars became incredible polite set pieces, fought between professional armies, with fantastically elaborate rules of honour and warfare to do with captives and the conduct of war. They had almost nothing to do with the people for whom the wars were fought and on whose territory they were being fought.

What I am saying in all of this is that there is this one tendency that as long as you have a 'steady state', in which nobody particularly wants, or has any reason, to change things very much, there will be violence, and it will be ritualised. This does not mean that nobody gets killed; it merely means that killing is reduced to a minimum. The question then becomes: when doesn't this work? In effect, I am really reversing the whole question about war and peace. It is not a matter of how terrible war is, wouldn't it be better to have peace? My question is, if you're going to have war anyway, what's the best kind of war to have? When it doesn't work is, I think, a matter for empirical research, and a lot of people are in fact working on this. It doesn't work when you get conquest, when you get huge population explosions, when people spill over from one territory into another; it doesn't work when you get displacements of people, or when the weapons of war outstrip the ritualisation of it.

So I want to conclude, I suppose, by saying that if we can't have peace, which is probably impossible, then perhaps the state to aim for is the state of contained or ritualised fighting, because this allows men to maximise those grandiose vainglorious and combative status-striving motives that they seem to like, and to minimise the damage that is brought about. If contemporary political leaders could count coup on each other, indulge in arm wrestling, or play a game of tiddlywinks, then we would be back in a human state, as it were, where conflicts and even violence could be organised and coped with, where—to get desperately back to my title—we could tap those inherent rules that are part of the nature of the beast, of the nature of fighting, rules that tend to make it an organised and structured aspect of human behaviour.

Rules as a Bridge between Speech and Action

ROGER LINDSAY

A tug-of-war is always an entertaining spectacle. It appeals to that sentiment somewhere between malice and humour, which finds enjoyment in the misfortunes of others; and from the outset we know that in a tug-of-war one side or the other must suffer misfortune. On a really good day both sides may collapse in disarray. When the rival teams are scholars, straining with all their might in opposing directions, the added promise of ruffled dignity does much to compensate for the fact that the tug-of-war is almost always intellectual in such cases. One such spectacle has recently presented itself on the borderline between linguistics and social psychology, where the protagonists are to be witnessed still, swaying uncertainly back and forth across the boundary.

It is natural and inevitable that there should be explanatory competition among the social sciences. The behavioural territory which each social science embraces overlaps to an uncertain extent with others and yet the explanatory constructs which each employs may be very different. Many psychologists, for example, still prefer to explain in terms of intelligence, much of the behaviour which sociologists account for in terms of social class. Another form of competition is generated by the mechanism of explanation itself, together with differential rates of development within the social sciences. Explanation frequently proceeds by productively comparing an unfamiliar system to a system which is already familiar, and it is tempting for workers within one social science to turn for an explanation of phenomena which are peripheral but within its own territory, to other social sciences within which the same phenomena, occupying a more central position, have received explanatory attention already. In the example considered at length in this paper, social psychologists have turned to linguistics for an explanation of some aspects of speech behaviour, and in polite reciprocation linguists have turned to social psychology for an explanation of performative utterances. The drawback of inter-disciplinary borrowing of this type is that too often the borrowed explanatory device, much like the rabbit introduced to Australia, succeeds too well and threatens indigenous fauna. Thus, for example, it is hard to accept the constructs of recent linguistics without also accepting its methodology, and yet if its rather narrow methodology is accepted as compatible with more orthodox procedures in experimental psychology (as it must be if recent linguistic accounts of syntactic and semantic aspects of language are to be exploited by social psychologists), then it becomes impossible to prevent the transplanted methodology from generating competing explanations for more classical areas within the host discipline, in this case explanations based on intuitions rather than public observation.

If upon this picture of explanations borrowed from linguistics striving to swallow up social psychology, we superimpose a picture of explanations borrowed from social psychology striving to swallow up linguistics, then the basic structure of the tug-of-war starts to emerge. There is even a rope of sorts connecting the two teams: neither of the explanatory transplants will work without extensive use of the concept of 'rule'. Accordingly, it is this concept we shall examine, secure in the knowledge that if it can be weakened only a little, we may have the satisfaction of seeing both teams collapse in confusion.

The expository tactics of this paper will involve three stages: Firstly, the two types of explanatory transplant, from action to language and from language to action, will be more fully described and illustrations given of their use. This will permit us to ascribe the views discussed to particular authors so that we may more readily see that the criticisms presented later are directed at men of flesh and not straw. Secondly, the different senses in which the term 'rule' is used will be briefly discussed. Lastly, considerations of logic and method will be adduced which suggest that the term 'rule' has little or no explanatory value in psychology.

The idea that some aspects of language behaviour can profitably be treated as extensions of action was first brought to the attention of philosophers by Austin (1962). Recently Searle (1970) has updated and elaborated Austin's views, and a number of linguistic theorists (McCawley, 1968; Ross, 1970) have shown themselves to be greatly taken with the idea that a performative verb underlies every grammatical utterance. Two dialectical moves are required in any attempt to explain language function in this way. Move one involves the abolition of any distinction between talking and doing, and move two involves the claim that if we need to specify the rules which constrain action to understand people's doings, then, given move one, we must specify a further set of rules to understand their sayings. Searle makes both moves in a single sentence: 'Speaking a language is engaging in a rule-governed form of behaviour' (Searle, 1970 : 22). Other authorities are less precipitous, but they do in a more timorous or leisurely fashion manifest their approval of both moves.

Austin distinguished six different sorts of act which are normally performed by a successful utterer. The phonetic, phatic, and rhetic acts will not be discussed in any detail here; subsequent work in phonology has demonstrated not only that the notion of a phonetic act is unnecessary for explanatory progress but also that it is unlikely that speech ever involves an utterer manipulating phonemes (Corcoran, 1971). The terms 'phatic' and 'rhetic' are acoustically barbarous, even for neologisms. It is also true that the label 'phatic act' is otiose; narrowly construed it appears to be synonymous with 'grammatical', and broadly construed it appears to be synonymous with 'sequencing'. Searle (1968) has argued convincingly that 'rhetic' acts are indistinguishable from a further Austinian action-category, namely 'locutionary acts'.

At a more microscopic level, a 'locutionary' act is performed when a phonetic act, a phatic act and a rhetic act are carried out in making an utterance with a 'more or less definite sense and reference' (Austin, 1962 : 93). Roughly, the locutionary component of a speech act conveys the meaning of the utterance. The 'illocutionary' component specifies the illocutionary force. Thus, if I command my dog to be seated, the locutionary component of the act informs us that it is sitting (as opposed to barking, staying, or any other canine activity) which the dog must perform to obey my command. The illocutionary component informs the dog (and the audience) that sitting is being *commanded* (rather than defined, used in a description, or any of the other things which a speaker may do). The 'perlocutionary' component of the speech act is the act performed in making the dog aware that it must seat itself if it is to retain my goodwill.

It is doubtful whether these distinctions are worth making. In an early review of Austin's (1962) book, Max Black suggested that 'In Pursuit of a Vanishing Distinction' would have been an apt subtitle for 'How to Do Things with Words' (Black, 1963). Similarly Searle (1970) argues that the study of meaning is not in principle distinct from the study of illocutionary force. Cohen concludes a critique of the notion of illocutionary force with the following words: 'What Austin calls the illocutionary force of an utterance is that aspect of its meaning which is either conveyed by its explicit performative prefix if it has one, or might have been so conveyed by the use of such an expression. Any attempt to prise off this aspect of meaning and regard it as something else leads to paradox and confusion' (1964 : 125). Perlocutionary acts are not linguistic events and so do not fall within the scope of a discussion of the extension of the term 'act' to speech behaviour. Suffice it to note that categorising the state of affairs created in the world by a succession of previous acts as itself an act of a speaker, is unlikely to be a productive step. Nor is any attempt to categorise the consequences of an act as a separate act of the performer.

Searle concurs with Austin's suggestion that it is fruitful to regard speakers as performing acts. The kit of distinctions which goes along with Searle's position is somewhat different from that of Austin. Searle, too, distinguishes three categories of speech act, but on his theory one type of act performed by the speaker is 'uttering', a second is 'referring' or 'predicating' and the third is a category which includes 'stating', 'questioning', 'ordering', and many other old favourites. These three types of act are not necessarily separable like, to use Searle's example, buying a ticket, boarding a train, and reaching one's destination. Rather they describe three actions carried out in doing one thing, just as in putting a cross on a ballot paper one may simultaneously perform the acts of voting and contributing to the success of the victorious candidate.

Whatever doubts there may be about what sorts of act are being performed in speaking, it is clear that to carry out this sort of analysis, language behaviour must be regarded as a rule-governed activity, and it is these rules which determine the success or 'felicity' of the things people do in talking (Austin, 1962). I shall return later to question the status of these rules and ask whether they really do have explanatory utility. First, though, I shall describe the team at the other end of the rope.

The converse form of explanatory transplant has its roots in envy. Social psychologists look over the fence at their colleagues in linguistics and allow themselves to be convinced that what they see is the most advanced of all the social sciences. Linguistic theorists have developed elaborate procedures of observation, description, and explanation (indeed linguistic theorists frequently use the term 'explanation' in a way which is quite unique in science), and it appears to some observers that they have made more explanatory progress in the last twenty years than most disciplines can cram into a century, once a-priorism has been relinquished.[1]

Some theorists of social science have gone beyond expressing admiration for linguistics, and have proposed that other social sciences should accept it as a model of what a developed social science should be. Harré and Secord (1972) provide one example of this position in their book, *The Explanation of Social Behaviour*. Ryan's (1970) book, *The Philosophy of the Social Sciences*, provides another. In a passage typical of writers who believe that the natural sciences are inappropriate models for the social sciences, and that explanations in the social sciences must take a different form, Ryan offers the view that 'the so-called behavioural sciences have only contrived to mimic the surface features of the physical sciences. They can detect the regularities of outward behaviour, but cannot account for its interior logic or organisation. Social behaviour is to be understood as rule-following behaviour rather than as causally regular behaviour' (: 126).

Even in this brief passage, the reader may detect some rather odd assumptions. In what sense, for example, are the social sciences unable to account for the interior logic or organisation of behaviour? Is Ryan simply telling us that the explanatory programme of psychology is not yet complete and that we 'cannot', as a matter of fact, account for the internal processes which underlie behaviour? Few will be surprised that after only a hundred years of scientific psychology, there are still many outstanding problems. It would have been sad indeed if physicists had abandoned their traditional forms of explanation in the mid-nineteenth century, on the grounds that physics had up to that point failed to account for the interior logic and organisation of the atom. A deeper sense of 'cannot' may be intended by Ryan. Perhaps he is suggesting that *in principle* a behaviourist methodology cannot account for events

1. Maclay (1971) has even claimed that two Kuhnian paradigm shifts have occurred in linguistics this century. Even ignoring the problems associated with distinguishing normal change in science from 'paradigm shifts', it is odd that the second of Maclay's paradigm shifts involves little more than a reversion to a prior *status quo*.

within the organism. Arguments of this sort are not easy to refute. In the last analysis 'stand and watch' may be the best reply. Columbus would never have reached America if he had spent his time arguing with those who held it to be impossible in principle. There are other reasons for optimism: one is that in some cases it *has* been possible to account, at least in part, for the 'interior logic or organisation' of behaviour on the basis of data which included only the regularities of outward behaviour. The area of concept learning in psychology offers a case in point (see, for example, Bruner et al. 1956; Bourne, 1966; Hunt et al., 1966; Trabasso and Bower, 1968; Kintsch, 1970), and certainly it is clear from research in such areas that theories and models of great predictive and explanatory power may be supported by behavioural data alone. It seems unlikely, to judge from areas where explanation is reasonably advanced, that introspection would have provided faster progress. One reason is that most of the control processes which regulate behaviour do not appear to be available to introspection.

A second rejoinder to Ryan involves an appeal to an analogy between men and computers. There is no doubt whatever that the 'interior logic and organisation' of a computer can, given time (and not too much of that for a small computer), be deduced solely from observation and manipulation of input-output regularities. Why should biological computers, be they men or rats, be different? And why, after all, should data other than those concerning behavioural regularities be relevant? The internal logic of a computer can be inferred from input-output regularities even if its output consists entirely of false descriptions of its own principles of operation. It is fortunate that this is true, for much of the output from human beings is of this form.

Finally, what if social psychology does abandon all attempts to explain social behaviour in causal terms? There will then remain room for some discipline which does investigate the causal implementation of the 'rules' which are alleged to underlie behaviour, and a new name will have to be invented for it. Why, if the search for causes differs from the search for rules, should those who search for causes be forced to change their habits or change their name? Why, instead, do we not rename the search for rules 'Social Jurisprudence' or 'Social Description'? It is instructive that many of those who seek to dissuade us from specifying causes by declaring the enterprise impossible are philosophers. It may be cynical to suggest a reason for their efforts. If philosophers can convince social scientists to abandon an empiricist methodology and espouse rationalism instead, it simultaneously becomes true that the skills of the philosopher become the skills which are necesary to conduct enquiry in social psychology, and true also that the philosopher instantly becomes equipped to carry on enquiries in social science without needing to acquire any knowledge of its techniques and procedures. Similarly, if Columbus and all subsequent navigators had allowed themselves to be persuaded that it was vain to put to sea, the relevant skills in discussions of long-distance navigation would still be those of the philosopher rather than the navigator.

The assumptions we have discussed reflect the negative side of the belief that the methods of linguistics are an appropriate model for explanation of action by social psychologists. The positive side usually involves two claims. Firstly, that the psychologist should broaden his concept of acceptable data to include intuitions of one sort or another, and secondly, that explanation in psychology importantly or exclusively consists in the specification of rules, in particular 'generative' rules. We shall now critically consider the use of rules as explanatory terms in psychology. This is the link between the two forms of explanatory transplant which have been described. Before doing so, however, it may be useful to consider some objections to reliance upon intuitions as data. One justification for this is that though a number of serious objections of this type do exist, no explicit statement of them has recently appeared. A second reason is that if we do not attach undue importance to intuitions as data in psychology, the use of rules as explanatory constructs appears somewhat less attractive.

In general there are three ways in which a social scientist may obtain information about behaviour. He may *observe* relevant behaviour, he may *elicit* relevant behaviour or he may *interrogate an informant* who claims to have observed relevant behaviour. All of these procedures are liable to distortions arising from observer bias and reactivity. Pure observation provides the simplest context in which to attempt to control these distortions. Observation alone, cannot, however, always discriminate causality from correlation, and may be extremely costly if the relevant behaviour has a low occurrence rate. Elicitation techniques (or experimental procedures) evade the special problems of observation, but multiply the dangers of reactive measures, and introduce the problem that the context in which behaviour is elicited may differ in important ways from the context in which it naturally occurs. Neither of these problems is insurmountable; reactive measures may be avoided, or the reactive bias measured or controlled. The claim that some variable which has not been controlled in the past is relevant to a piece of behaviour is not an objection to experimentation, but rather the specification of a new experiment.

The special problems associated with informants are not so easy to evade, and they become progressively more crippling if we allow the informant to become identical with the behaver (about whom information is given, or the interrogator who asks the informant the questions, or both). It is usual in linguistics for all three roles to be played by the same individual, though this is by no means necessary (and should be avoided whenever possible). Informant bias and its interaction with other role requirements will be discussed separately here for expository convenience, but it must be borne in mind that the three classes of bias in combination undoubtedly interact positively. We shall also restrict our consideration to those procedures which involve the presentation of relevant segments of behaviour to an informant who then judges it to be acceptable or not. Such procedures are typical in recent linguistics; the assumption behind them being that a native speaker (or actor) has access to an internal source of evidence called 'intuition', on which he bases his judgement.

This assumption has two crucial weaknesses. Firstly, we do not know what the relationship is between the state of the informant's intuitions and his responses. We *do* know, however, that various factors operate to prevent responses from reflecting intuition alone; informants often do not take the interrogation seriously, and may lie or reply perversely. They may also make honest mistakes, or attempt to please the investigator by saying what they think he wishes to hear. Also, in an interrogation situation a sentence (or piece of behaviour) is 'uttered' (or emitted) but not used (there is invariably an arbitrary relationship between the sentence and the socio-physical setting in which it is uttered). There is a wealth of psychological evidence to show that the interpretation of a sentence (let alone judgements of its acceptability) depends upon the context (Light and Carter-Sobell, 1970). Furthermore, if many sentences are presented, then judgements will not be independent, both because of response bias (it is doubtful if informants are free from bias towards either 'yes' or 'no' responses to start with; there are few tasks in which they are), and because memory information available for interpretation of later sentences depends upon the content of those presented earlier. These problems are frequently intensified by a failure to exercise proper control over presentation variables. Many linguists, for example, present sample sentences in lists arranged in increasing order of anomalousness (e.g. Lakoff, 1971 :

332). Secondly, even if response factors could be eliminated, there would be a stimulus problem; there is no way of ascertaining the relationship between the strength of the evidence available to the subject via his intuitions, and the true acceptability of the sentence. An analogy may make these points clearer. Other contexts in which subjects make yes/no judgements include signal detection studies and recognition memory studies. Smaller bias effects are likely in studies of this type as judgements of sentence acceptability probably involve more complex processes. Even in tasks such as these, the functions relating the presence or absence of a signal or the familiarity of an item to responses are extremely complex and involve sophisticated decision processes. In psychophysical studies or studies of recognition memory it is possible to calibrate the human operator, but only because we can examine responses to known stimulus values. In psychophysics we can compare whether someone reports a signal with whether or not one was presented; in studies of recognition memory claims that an item is familiar can be checked against which stimuli have already been presented.

There are no equivalent methods for ascertaining the acceptability value of a sentence or action segment. When the informant is neither the behaver, nor the interrogator, his judgements are associated with two large but unspecified error components. We do not know the relationship between the bias component of acceptability/unacceptability judgements and the quantity or degree of anomouslessness, nor do we know the relationships of such factors as incentive, motivation, reinforcement or prior experience to judgements based on intuitions. If judgements based on intuitions are at all like judgements based on other forms of internal evidence (such as hypothetical 'neural magnitudes' or 'familiarity') then there are good reasons to believe that they are neither simply nor linearly related to the properties of sentences which they are supposed to reflect. At best the use of intuitions as data is not an alternative to empirical investigation, but a poor example of it.

If the behaver is identical with the informant then the error component of uncertain size is likely to increase. If we ask a man to produce a sentence which violates some rule, then it is likely that his judgements of whether it is acceptable will be influenced by the processes involved in generating the instance. Conversely, requiring an informant to judge or describe his own verbal output is likely to alter his output. Finally, serious distortions are likely to occur if the interrogator and informant are one. It is hard to believe that acceptability judgements are unaffected by knowledge of hypotheses under test or firm beliefs about the rules underlying performance. Rosenthal (1968) has discussed biases of this form in psychology, often in cases where the methodology is less risky than that in linguistics.

It is now time to turn to the concept of 'rule'. We have been introduced to the team of linguists, who propose that ⌊speech is really a special sort of rule-governed action,⌋and to the team of social psychologists, who believe that actions are socially meaningful only because they are based on the same sort of rules as language. We have also seen that even if the concept of 'rule' is strong enough to bear the strain which both teams impose upon it, each of them still has serious problems—the linguist because the consequences of assimilating action to speech may be only an extension of the domain he cannot explain; the social psychologists because an acceptance of the methodology of linguistics requires the acceptance of discovery procedures which have a large but unspecifiable error component. There seems to be no way in which this error component can be eliminated or measured, as can the error components of more traditional measures in psychology.

The word 'rule' has many meanings. We shall not consider uses of the word as a verb or as a concrete noun in this essay. Even within these limitations there are quite a selection of uses from which to choose. Perhaps we should start by eliminating those senses which are least likely to be useful in psychology or linguistics. One such sense is rules as *regulations* (cf. Black, 1962). Rules of this type include laws, statutes and school rules. The distinguishing features of regulations are that they have dates and authors. We can always sensibly ask who made them and when they were instituted. They are likely to have a stipulated or understood domain as well. It would be absurd, for instance, to prosecute a leopard escaping from a zoo for travelling at more than seventy miles an hour on a motorway. In other cases the domain of the regulation may be less obvious. To quote a stock example of philosophers, it may take a court case to decide whether harbour regulations apply to flying boats and hovercraft. Few would wish to argue that rules of social action are of this type.

A person may also be said to be acting in accordance with rules when he follows *directions*, such as those associated with making a cake or putting a plug on a new electric fire. There is an obvious distinction between rules of this sort which are followed to attain a certain end, and regulations which are backed by a sovereign agent of some sort who has the power to insist, on pain of the application of sanctions, that a class of organisms or entities behaves in a certain way. Directions are guides for producing a desired result, and Black (1962) points out that this feature of directions means that it must always be possible to evaluate directions by asking questions like 'how is the quality of my cake affected by the omission of flour?' It is clear that syntax does not vary according to the purposes for which we use language; we do not use one set of linguistic rules when we argue with a traffic warden and another when we talk to friends; nor does lexical choice and arrangement become completely haphazard in idle conversation. It is unlikely that this sense of 'rules' has more than peripheral relevance to explanations of language behaviour and social performance.

A third sense of 'rule' can be used with reference to moral and prudential rules. Various other distinctions within this category, though valuable in other contexts, are an unnecessary refinement here. Rules of prudence would include such maxims as 'Neither a borrower nor a lender be', and moral rules embrace exhortations such as 'Love thy neighbour as thyself' as well as negative strictures like 'Do not covert thy neighbour's wife'. Prudential rules are something like directions but the goal to which they direct one is not easy to specify except in a vague way (e.g. 'follow this rule if you wish to live a good life'). Moral rules are closer to regulations, but no particular sanctions are prescribed in advance, and so special agency is designated to apply whatever sanctions there may be (such as social disapproval, disbarment from the club). A characteristic feature of moral and prudential rules is that, like regulations, they are *normative*. The language of 'oughts' and 'shoulds' is appropriate when an appeal is made to normative rules, and the suggestion is always present that their violation is not only foolish, but wicked or culpable. By contrast, directions are *descriptive*; they merely invite us to achieve an end in the most effective way.

A fourth type of rule, which is also descriptive, seems to have been noticed earliest by Immanuel Kant, though Searle (1970) has recently redirected attention to rules of this type. This fourth category of rule is the *constitutive* rule, which lays down criteria for identifying and reidentifying events of a particular type. The rules which specify what counts as a 'goal' in rugby, or 'checkmate' in chess, are rules of this sort. This sort of rule is undoubtedly relevant to the description of behaviour, telling us, as constitutive rules do, whether a speaker has successfully given a command, or participated in a greeting ritual. Such rules will not, however, *explain* behaviour. They will not tell us *how* a speaker uttered a command. Similarly an observer familiar only with the notion of 'goal' would make an exceedingly bad football commentator.

The fifth type of rule, descriptive and a little closer to explanation, is the *procedural* rule. Familiar examples include '*i* before *e*, except after *c*', and Fleming's Right and Left Hand Rules in physics (which allow the direction to be calculated, of induced current, the direction of a magnetic field or the direction in which that field is moved relative to a coil, given that the remaining two terms are known).

Waismann (1965) illustrates the procedural use of rules by suggesting two ways in which one might play chess. One method is that followed conventionally, where players learn the game and the rules are only relevant to the game in so far as they provide backing for challenges of illegal moves, justifications of wrongly challenged moves, and so on. The second method would probably only be employed by an eccentric. Here the player does not need to know the game. He might, for example, decide randomly between moves which the rules did not proscribe, each time it was his turn. In this second case a complete description of the player's behaviour would require mention of the rules consulted on each move. Even a causal account of chess-playing behaviour of this sort would need to refer to the version of the rules of chess that had been consulted during play. Consultation of an external version of the rules, or allowing a readily verbalisable internalised version to guide behaviours, is typical of a novice at any skill. The evidence suggests, however, that it is a necessary precondition for fluid and automatic behaviour that the performer has progressed beyond this stage (see Holding, 1966). Although the rules may assist acquisition, there is still little reason to believe that they explain expert performance.

The last type of rule, and one which is central to explanation in linguistics, is a *generative* rule. The sense of 'generative' employed here is borrowed from logic and mathematics. In this sense the definitions of variables and operators, together with the axioms for a logical system, generate the well-formed formulae for that system. An algorithm may similarly be said to 'generate' those of its outputs which can be derived by applying it to permissible input values. In linguistics the base rules, transformation rules, semantic rules and phonological rules are said to 'generate' the sentences of a language. It is important to notice, as Chomsky (1971) points out, that generation is not to be construed as a process, but as a stative, logical relationship. To 'generate' the sentences of a language in this sense, a set of elements which may or may not be rules and terminal vocabulary items merely has to possess a unique and specifiable relationship to the set of sentences. Used in this way, rules provide a convenient method of characterising the sentences of a language. Convenient summaries are, however, not the same things as explanations. The question of *how* a mechanism (be it electronic or biological) follows such rules in practice remains unanswered.

The suspicion may be growing in the mind of the reader that none of these senses of the term 'rule' is likely to explain very much in science. A more detailed consideration of some of the distinctions offered already will undoubtedly help to foster this feeling. One distinction we have discussed is that between rules which are normative and those which are descriptive. Regulative rules and moral and prudential rules are normative, while directions, constitutive, procedural and generative rules are usually held to be descriptive.

Some authors have argued that the rules which underlie and explain regularities in speech and social behaviour are also normative. One example of such an author is Vendler (1967), who says that 'a set of rules may describe a game, but only inasmuch as it prescribes how the game is to be played. Linguistics, as I have emphasised, is an empirical science, and its findings, the rules of language, are contingent truths. Yet this is only half the story, and we have to add that a rule has a normative as well as a descriptive aspect; it describes the *correct* performance' (: 24). Another example of this view may be found in Black's *The Labyrinth of Language*. Black roundly claims that 'if the users of a language were not trained to recognise certain ways of speaking as right, correct or grammatical, and others as wrong, human communication would be a more chancey and less tightly organized affair than it is' (: 59). This assertion is an odd one in its own right (cf. if God did not exist, the universe would be more chancey and less tightly organised that it is; if rice puddings were not mammals, human communication would be more chancey . . . etc.), but at least it is clear that in Black's belief rules underlie language performance, and those rules are prescriptive (Black, 1968).

There are three good reasons why the position adopted by Vendler, Black and others like them is unacceptable: one is that people's speech behaviour differs and it is not clear whose standards of correctness we should take. The second is that normative rules are redundant, as regularities in speech behaviour can be explained without their help. The third is that normative rules acquire sanctions to back them, and yet it is unclear what sanctions are applied when people use language irregularly. The problem posed by differences in speech behaviour among members of a community arises in two forms: sometimes it appears directly as the problem of which groups of individuals should be taken as arbiters of correct standards. The view that language rules are prescriptive holds an attraction for philosophers, due to the tacit assumption that it is philosophers themselves who know what is correct. This view is more often propounded with respect to semantic rules than with respect to phonological or syntactic rules. In its most severe form it leads to the suggestion that the meaning of a sentence is actually equivalent to the beliefs of some status group (e.g. leading scientists under Neurath's 'protocol-statement' theory, Urmson, 1965). Milder versions produce a rather arrogant assumption that particular beliefs held by the author are guaranteed by the rules of language. A set of rules impeccably supported by the author's intuitions are then trotted out and shown to tally exactly with the author's beliefs. Lakoff (1971) provides a good example of this. First he argues that some verbs impose selectional restrictions on the types of subject they may 'legitimately' take. The verb 'talk' is one example of such a verb. This hypothesis is then 'proved' by presenting sentences in which a verb requiring an animate subject is appended to an inanimate subject, and an asterisk is assigned to the whole sentence. Thus, to take a slightly modified example from Lakoff (1971),

*'The man who was killed yesterday is talking'

is alleged to be anomalous and to support Lakoff's theory. In this way all those who are spiritualists, or who believe that life persists after the demise of the fleshly containers in which persons reside, are not only seen as accepting erroneous beliefs but also as ignorant of the rules of their native language.

Fortunately no great harm is done by these individuals who believe that only the speech behaviour of their own or another social group is correct, and that their own beliefs are built into the rules of language, provided that not too many people believe them. Such positions are only likely to win converts from among those who already have highly similar beliefs. More generally, it appears that speakers of a language model their speech behaviour not on the pronouncements of linguists or philosophers but rather on the speech behaviour of social groups which they admire or emulate.

The problem of whose standards of correctness a prescriptivist should accept also arises as the question: what counts as 'a language'?

Thus, for example, standard English may be defined so as to exclude Cockney on the grounds that Cockney speakers do not adhere to the rules of standard English. Extreme versions of this position accept that each speaker has a unique 'idiolect' which has its own rules. Instead of abandoning talk of rules when regularities break down, a different set of rules is attributed to each individual.

The problem of how prescriptivists decide whose behaviour is correct is not confined to language behaviour. Becker (1963) has observed that

> all social groups make rules and attempt at some time and under some circumstances to enforce them: Social rules define situations and the kinds of behaviour appropriate to them, specifying some action as right and others as wrong. When the rule is enforced the person who is supposed to have broken it may be seen as a special kind of person, one who cannot be trusted to move by the rules agreed on by the group; he is an outsider. But the person who is thus labelled as an outsider may have a very different view of the matter. He may not accept the rule by which he is being judged, and he may not regard those who judge him as either competent or legitimately entitled to do so. The rule breaker may feel his judges are outsiders (: 128).

Some readers may suspect that this rather unseemly game of 'I'm right and you're wrong!' . . . 'No, I'm right and you're wrong!' is unlikely to lead to productive advance in science. Even if it is conceded, however, that one set of rules and beliefs is correct, and all the others wrong, even though there is no way of discovering which set is correct, the problem of sanctions remains. What are the sanctions which apply when linguistic rules are broken? What persons or agencies impose these sanctions, and who by prior agreement or contract gave them the right and power to do so? Unless native speakers are aware of the answers to these questions it is unlikely that the sanctions will be effective. If, as prescriptive theories must maintain, sanctions for rule violation are necessary to explain regularities in social behaviour then it must be concluded that where there are no sanctions, there must be rule-violation, and thus that rules have no relevance to statistically unusual speech-patterns.

A sensible rejoinder is that language deviance generates its own sanctions. Unless we observe the norms of speech behaviour and social interaction, our fellows will not understand what we say or do. This is quite true of course, but is hardly a reason for believing that rules are necessary to explain regularities in social behaviour. The regularities in the way a man goes to work are a product of the interaction between his ability to solve spatial problems and his desire to reach his goal. He may choose a similar route each day, not because a rule says that only that route is correct, but rather because he knows that other routes require additional time or effort. When a speaker knows that a regular pattern of speech behaviour exists in a community, he knows also that the adoption of this pattern of speech will maximise his chances of trouble-free communication. For, given no further information, this pattern of behaviour is more likely to be the one that a hearer has learnt than any other. Arbitrary regularities in behaviour are to be expected in any situation involving communication between mechanisms that are capable of learning. One piece of empirical evidence which suggests that people speak in predictable ways so that other people can understand them, rather than to avoid unspecifiable sanctions for the violation of unspecifiable rules, is that fluent speakers are frequently able to switch from one set of regularities to another, according to the social context (Leech, 1975).

The arguments we have examined so far suggest that the notion of prescriptive rules of social behaviour is unhelpful. It should not be concluded, however, that descriptive rules do not have problems associated with them. The category of descriptive rules, it will be recalled, includes directions, constitutive rules, rules as procedures and generative rules. There is no question that most of these types of rules offer elegant and useful ways of describing regularities in behaviour. The question then centres on whether or not they have any *explanatory* utility. Are rules only a form of behavioural taxonomy, or are they part of a hypothetical process underlying behaviour? Quine (1972) offers a similar distinction between rules which are 'behaviour-fitting' and rules which are 'behaviour guiding'. He describes his distinction in the following way:

> My distinction between 'guiding' and 'fitting' is, you see, the
> obvious and flat-footed one. Fitting is a matter of true description;
> guiding is a matter of cause and effect. Behaviour fits a rule
> whenever it conforms to it, whenever the rule truly describes
> the behaviour, but behaviour is not guided by a rule unless the

behaver knows the rule and can state it. This behaviour *observes* the rule (: 442).

Most astronomers now accept that the explanations of patterns of celestial motion and planetary orbits are provided by classical or relativistic mechanics. Astronomers at the time of Ptolemy believed that because rules could be used to describe and even predict the motions of the heavenly bodies, such rules must compel the planets and stars to behave in the way they do. Descriptive rules may be used quite neutrally to characterise regularities in the behaviour of both animate and inanimate objects. The attraction of animism as an explanatory device in science has almost completely dwindled away by now, and few would admit to believing that rules are causally involved in even the most regular behaviour of objects which are inanimate. If all regular behaviour can be described by rules, and if the rules are clearly not a part of the process underlying regular behaviour in the case of inanimate objects, but only a form of description, then why should it be supposed that the rules are a part of the process underlying regular behaviour in any cases at all? Animism has not yet been completely extirpated in psychology. Even so, it should be clear that some evidence, additional to the regularity itself, must be provided before it is necessary, or even tempting, to believe that rules provide anything more than a taxonomy of behavioural regularities.

Quine (1972) suggests that in second language teaching it is possible to teach novices any one of a large set of extensionally equivalent grammars of English (that is, grammars which account for the same subset of English sentences). Behaviour will *fit* the formulations of the rules provided by all of the grammars, but it will only be guided by the one actually taught. Again, the same moral: a good fit between rules and behaviour proves only that the rule-maker had closely observed behaviour when formulating his rules. It does not guarantee that the behaver is following any rules; nor, if he is, does it tell us which rules he is following.

The extra evidence demanded by Quine is that the behaver be capable of articulating the rules which *guide* his behaviour. Strictly speaking, ability to articulate a rule which fits behaviour is not a sufficient condition for saying that the rule forms a part of behaviour. It is possible to program a computer, for example, to provide on request an account of a program which would produce its own input-output regularities but which is different from the program which in fact underlies its performance. If human being have a need or desire to formulate descriptions of their own performance it is easily possible that they should be able to articulate rules which *fit* their performace without those rules having any part at all in the *production* of their performance. The fact that the ability to articulate a rule which fits behaviour is not uncommon is no justification for the attribution of a causal role to rules. Better evidence would be the complete absence of cases of speech or action where there was no related ability to specify a rule which fitted the behaviour, or better still, evidence that differences between the various versions of rule which behavers formulate were reflected in differences in the appropriate behaviour. It is interesting that the methodology of linguistics assumes that all speakers of a natural language will agree in judgements of which strings are correctly formed sentences of their native language and which are not. The most respected linguistic theorists disagree among themselves as to what the rules are which generate English sentences. If the rules a behaver articulates really do underlie his behaviour then the linguistic behaviour of different linguistic theorists must differ and there is no possibility of agreement based upon intuitions in linguistics. On the other hand, if agreement based upon intuitions is possible, then linguistic behaviour must be independent of the versions of a rule which a behaver formulates, and so must merely fit such a rule.

Even if the ability to articulate a rule on request were a sufficient condition for the assertion that a corresponding rule underlay performance, rule theorists would still have to face the fact that most speakers are not able to formulate rules which fit their behaviour or rules which specify their social actions. Some rule theorists have tried to argue that only *some* agents need to be able to specify a rule for it to underlie everyone's behaviour. While others have tried to argue that only those who can cite the rules are real people. Gumb (1972) is an example of the latter class. He says, 'There are degrees of personhood. The more linguistic acts a speaker can perform, the more readily he can cite the rules of his language as reasons for his behaviour, and the more he strives to teach the language to the young, the more fully does he realise his personhood' (: 129).

Neither of these alternatives deserves much comment. If the ability to articulate a rule is supposed to be a necessary condition for saying that a man's behaviour is guided by a rule, then the existence of even one man who cannot articulate the rules is evidence that behaviour may occur even when rules do not guide it. Such cases are in fact more

common and more interesting than cases of individuals who can
formulate rules. We have already found that rule theorists frequently
find themselves tempted into believing that those who hold different
opinions are ignorant of the rules of language or the rules of behaviour.
Gumb gets close to suggesting that rule theorists are the only real
persons, or at least a particularly elevated type of person. Quite apart
from its social repugnance, this doctrine is quite unacceptable. It
leaves quite unanswered the question of how non-persons speak, and it
provides an unembroidered illustration of the 'no-true-Scotsman'
fallacy. Compare:

No Scotsman goes to funerals without his kilt
But Hamish went to a funeral without his kilt
Ah, well, no *true* Scotsman etc . . .

No one can talk without being able to articulate rules
But Lindsay can talk and is unable to articulate rules
Ah, well no *true* person, etc. . . .

In logic, unlike war, the formation of a perfect circle is rarely a good
method of defence. Gumb's position is not psychologically plausible
either. In cases where it is possible to show that rules are being used in
performance, such use of rules is usually a mark of the novice, not the
skilled performer. Incidentally, is it not entirely certain that the
ability to articulate the rule is a *necessary* condition for behaviour
being guided by that rule; Black's example of 'no two chess pieces
may simultaneously occupy the same square', is a rule which chess
players almost always observe, but rarely list among the rules of chess.

Anticipating these problems, many rule-theorists have rejected the
articulation criterion, and have plumped instead for a criterion based
on the behaver's recognition ability, claiming that if a behaver can
recognise a formulation of a rule when he hears it, or recognise breaches
of it when he observes them, then his behaviour must be guided by the
relevant rule.

The requirement that a behaver be able to recognise a formulation of
the rules which guide his behaviour is normally relaxed somewhat in
the face of the fact that most behavers, even in our own culture, are
not readily able to comprehend the complex rules which theorists
propose, let alone recognise them as descriptions or familiar components of their own behaviour. Instead, it may be suggested that if

someone were taught enough linguistics, or enough psychology, he would then recognise some rule as guiding his own behaviour. This view is also mistaken. Imagine that a computer was programmed to argue about linguistics, and that under some circumstances it could be convinced that it was wrong, and the views of its interlocutor correct. It might easily be possible to convince the computer that a particular set of rules accounted best for its own output. The snag is that the production of this sort of conviction is quite a different process from making the computer aware of, or able to report, the true details of its program. Similarly if we take a native from the shores of a Polynesian island or the wilds of North Oxford, and after giving him an extensive grounding in linguistics, are able to convince him by the normal methods of argumentation within the subject that some rule is the most economical, or elegant, or best on whatever criteria are used, the fact that we are able to convince him according to such public criteria provides no additional guarantee that this rule guides his own private behaviour. Public criteria can only guarantee the fit.

The ability to recognise infractions or breaches as a criterion fares no better. How can we be sure that 'unacceptability' reports or 'bizarreness' reactions are responses to a rule-infraction rather than to the characteristics of a statistically unusual piece of behaviour. If there is no way of telling when a person's behaviour is causally related to a rule, then there cannot be a way of telling when it is causally related to a rule-infraction either, as rule-infractions can only be specified once the rule which guides behaviour is known. Indeed, unless some rules which guide behaviour can be identified, there is no reason for supposing that there are any connections whatever between rules and bizarreness reactions or rules and reports of unacceptability.

The application of sanctions has sometimes been regarded as the *sine qua non* of rule-infractions. Sanctions refers of course to the negative reinforcement applied by our fellows when we break rules. Negative reinforcement, however, is also applied on many other occasions. Identification of the subset of occasions on which the label 'sanction' is appropriate presupposes the isolation of relevant rules. Sanctions are in any event only relevant to prescriptive rules, and as we have seen one cannot plausibly argue that the rules of language are prescriptive.

Teachability has been suggested as a criterion for behaviour governed by rules. Gumb (1972) claims, for example, that 'it is a truism to say that instructors teach students second languages, and that children learn to speak—that they learn to generate grammatical utterances by conforming to the rules of language—by following the example of their elders and being corrected by them' (: 38). It is unfortunately true, though not a truism, that many truisms are false. The fact that language can be taught by rules does not imply that language must be so taught, and it certainly does not imply that rules are always involved in language processing. In fact it implies very little other than that rules provide an efficient way of transmitting information about behaviour.

Some rule-theorists concede that a behaver has no privileged access to the processes which regulate his own behaviour, they argue that behavioural regularities themselves may provide sufficient evidence for the postulation of a rule which guides it. Black (1962) provides one example, Collett (this volume) another. If Martians were to land in England they would soon realise that there is a rule requiring vehicles to travel on the left of roads. It is an important feature of the example cited in support of this position that the behaviour to be explained is entirely arbitrary. Rules may be plausibly invoked because there is no other possible explanation. We cannot assume from the outset that language behaviour or social behaviour is arbitrary in this way. It is doubtful if descriptive rules ever explain arbitrary behaviour of this type. Why, after all, should everyone behave in the same way, if there are no sanctions for failing to do so? If descriptive rules are to be invoked then they should only be used as a last resort, when all other attempts at explanation have failed—just as any claim that a sequence is arbitrary can be accepted only when every other possible dependency has been eliminated. None of these criteria are acceptable. Rules provide a convenient format for a taxonomy of complex behavioural events. There is no reason to suppose that they play any causal role in behavioural processes. It is indeed ironic that Chomsky, who thought that he had progressed beyond taxonomic linguistics, will primarily be remembered for the development of procedures for the systematic classification of sentences.

Various attempts have been made to defend the use of rules as explanatory devices. That of Gumb (1972) is probably the most thorough, if not the most persuasive. Gumb's primary mistake is to misidentify the threat against which he is defending. He remarks at one point, for example, that the behaviourist 'does not establish an *a priori* case showing that the concept *Linguistic Rule* is incoherent' (: 66). Later he concludes that 'conceptual arguments presented by the behaviourists do not establish grounds for banning the term "rule" from linguistic theories' (: 127). The issue is not whether the term 'linguistic rule' should be banned but rather whether it is useful in science, and particularly whether rules are part of the world to be explained or only useful techniques for representing some forms of data. Such words as 'banning' are more likely to feature in the vocabulary of the prescriptivist. Nor is it necessary to suppose that the term 'linguistic rule' is 'incoherent'; rather, that like all other terms, it may be used in ways which are unhelpful. It is unhelpful to suppose that rules are in the mind of the behaver.

Gumb defends rule theories against four arguments: the first is that rules are evaluative. This objection is rightly dismissed. The second objection is that natural language is not a rigid system and cannot be reduced to a set of rules. Gumb's reply to this is that behavioural or linguistic rules define not actual language but an idealised system. 'I will not repeat here', he says, 'the many arguments that have demonstrated the great value of idealization and formalizations in science' (: 61). The introduction of the notion of formalisation as equivalent to idealisation is neither relevant nor justified. The fallacy in Gumb's reply rests on the assumption that because idealisation is sometimes necessary in science, there is no need to justify it on particular occasions. If we look more carefully at uses of idealisation in physics, it soon becomes apparent that they are acceptable only when they are justified by an improvement in our ability to predict the behaviour of physical systems. Not only do idealised rules of language and behaviour fail to increase the predictability of relevant behaviour but, in order to preserve hypothesised rules from instant falsification by behavioural fact, we must also be prepared to allow the distinction between 'competence' and 'performance'. Idealised rules are not even intended to predict performance, so there is no defence on the grounds that they enable us to do it better. Instead of offering a justification on the grounds of utility, Gumb argues that an account of language behaviour in terms of rules 'is superior to those in terms of *mere* habits' (: 60). No real justification is provided for this assertion. We must decide for ourselves whether habits are more or less 'mere' than rules. My own inclination is to believe that either term offers only a redescription of behavioural regularities requiring explanation. It is interesting, however, that where there are reasons for some regularity in behaviour, then rules are superfluous elements of its explanation, and where there are no reasons it is hard to see why people follow the rule apart from 'mere habit'.

The third objection to the suggestion that rules have explanatory utility closely resembles the position defended in this essay. Gumb's imaginary objector, a rather ponderous and unsubtle behaviourist, suggests that rules are parts of theories, or descriptions of languages, not of processes in the heads of speakers. Paul Ziff is taken as typical of this position when he says that 'To argue therefore that there must be rules in natural language is like arguing that roads must be red if they correspond to red lines of a map' (Ziff, 1960 : 38). This 'paradoxical assertion' (Gumb, 1972 : 63) is rejected by Gumb on two grounds. One is that 'linguistic rules *can* be taught' (: 63). It is not of course disputed that rule-formulation may assist second language learning, or the later stages of first-language learning. Second, 'competent speakers generally agree on whether or not a rule-formulation codifies their linguistic behaviour' (: 63). The rub of course lies in the 'competence'. As Gumb goes on to admit, 'the linguist cannot always rely on obtaining formulations of rules from speakers, because some speakers, especially those who have not fully realized their personhood, may not be able to formulate the rules readily and they may be mistaken' (: 65). It is probably not necessary to offer a list of the errors which this claim illustrates, but briefly we should note that it renders Gumb's claim circular. It proves only that some individuals can formulate rules which fit behaviour, and quite unfairly questions whether those of us who do not accept that these rules are part of our own performance are even worth calling people. Finally it begs the question, why, if non-people can manage without rules, everyone else cannot.

As a last desperate manoeuvre, Gumb's behaviourist tries rejecting rules because they refer to mental episodes, which, at least on a Cartesian model, cannot interact with physical systems and so cannot be part of behavioural processes. If there were some reason to suppose that rules *are* mental episodes, then this objection might be a difficult one for the rule theorist. As it is, he may avoid the behaviourist's objection by claiming that linguistic rules do not refer to mental episodes, but instead are simply a means of representing data. Were the rule-theorist to make this claim, he would probably be correct.

The scenario for the rather sorry struggle that we described in the introduction to this essay is now complete. Each side has its feet firmly placed in a position which is not really worth occupying. The link between them which must take the weight of their demands is the notion of a rule. It is clear that this link will not withstand the strain imposed by either side. Both must surely collapse, but as a result of the flimsiness of the instrument by which they seek to bring about the downfall of others.

A disclaimer may be in order at this point. It has not been argued in this essay that rules are not scientifically useful. Nor has it been argued that there is any reason why linguistic theorists should seek explanation at a deeper level than rules can provide. It may well be no part of linguistics to specify processes. What is beyond doubt is that the specification of behavioural processes is part of the task of psychology. Newell (1967 : 207) has already stated the reason for this claim in commenting on work by Bourne, who has argued that description of concept-attainment in terms of rules provides adequate explanation. I cannot improve upon Newell's words:

> Let me summarize my reaction to Bourne's alternative that we can consider human beings as rule-followers without asking after the processes that enable those rules to be followed. Bourne is logically justified, there's no necessity to postulate processes, yet it is a failure to grasp an opportunity, for the processes are there. One can find mechanism for producing the light that shines from the stars, one can find the mechanism for photosynthesis, one can find the mechanism for sickle-cell anaemia, one can find the mechanism for inflation, and one can expect to find the mechanism that enables an organism to follow learned complex rules.

References

Altman, S.A. Sociobiology of Rhesus monkeys. II: Stochastics of social communication. *Journal of Theoretical Biology*, 1965, **8**, 490–522.

Argyle, M. *Social Interaction*. London: Methuen, 1969.

Argyle, M. *Bodily communication*. London: Methuen, 1975.

Argyle, M. and Little, B. Do personality traits affect behaviour? *Journal for the Theory of Social Behaviour*, 1971, **I**, 1–35.

Argyle, M., Salter, V., Nicholson, H., Williams, M. and Burgess, P. The communication of inferior and superior attitudes by verbal and non-verbal signals. *British Journal of Social and Clinical Psychology*, 1970, **9**, 222–31.

Austin, J.L. *How to do things with words*. Oxford: Oxford University Press, 1962.

Bailey, F.G. (ed.), *Stratagems and spoils*. Oxford: Blackwell, 1969.

Bales, R.F. Interaction and equilibrium. In A.P. Hare, E.F. Borgatta & R.F. Bales (eds.), *Small groups*. New York: Knopf, 1955.

Barth, F. *Models of social organisation*. London: Royal Anthropological Institute (Occasional paper No. 23), 1966.

Bartlett, F. *Remembering*. Cambridge: Cambridge University Press, 1932.

Beattie, J.H.M. On understanding ritual. In B. Wilson (ed.) *Rationality*. Oxford: Blackwell, 1970.

Becker, H. *Outsiders*. New York: Free Press, 1963.

Bell, D.R. The idea of a social science. *The Aristotelian Society,* Supplementary Volume XLI, 1967.

Bergson, H. *The two sources of morality and religion* (trans. R. Ashley Audra & C. Brereton). London: Macmillan, 1935.

Bierstedt, R. *The social order.* New York: McGraw-Hill, 1963.

Black, M. *Models and metaphors.* Ithaca: Cornell University Press, 1962.

Black, M. Austin on performatives. *Philosophy,* 1963, **38,** 217–226.

Black, M. *The labyrinth of language.* New York: Mentor Publishers, 1968.

Bloom, L. *Language development; Form and function in emerging grammars.* Cambridge, Mass.: MIT Press, 1971.

Bourne, L.E. *Human conceptual behaviour.* Boston: Allyn and Bacon, 1966.

Bowerman, M. Learning to talk: a cross-linguistic study of early syntactic development with special reference to Finnish. Unpublished doctoral dissertation, Harvard University, 1970.

Brackbill, Y. The use of social reinforcement in conditioning smiling. In Y. Brackbill & G.C. Thompson (eds.), *Behaviour in infancy and early childhood.* New York: Free Press, 1967.

Bradley, F.H. *Ethical studies.* Oxford: Clarendon Press, 1876.

Braybrooke, D. Taking liberties with the concept of rules. *Monist,* 1968, **52** (3), 329–58.

Brown, R. *Social Psychology.* Glencoe, Illinois: Free Press, 1965.

Brown, R. *A first language; the early stages.* Cambridge, Mass.: Harvard University Press, 1973.

Brown, R. and Berko, J. Word association and the acquisition of grammar. *Child Development,* 1960, **31,** 1–14.

Brown, R. and Gilman, A. The pronouns of power and solidarity. In T.A. Sebeok (ed.), *Style in language.* Cambridge: Technology Press, 1960.

Bruner, J.S. Nature and uses of immaturity. *American Psychologist,* 1972, **27,** 687–708.

Bruner, J.S. Organisation of early skilled action. In M.P.M. Richards (ed.), *The integration of the child into a social world.* Cambridge: Cambridge University Press, 1974.

Bruner, J.S., Goodnow, J.J. and Austin, G.A. *A study of thinking.* New York: Wiley, 1956.

Burton, R. *Personal narrative of a pilgrimage to Al-Madinah and Meccah.* New York: Dover Publications, 1964 (orig. 1855).

176 REFERENCES

Cazden, C.B. Play with language and metalinguistic awareness: one dimension of language experience. Paper presented at the Second Lucy Sprague Mitchell Memorial Conference at the Bank Street College of Education, 19 May 1973.

Chomsky, N. *Syntactic Structures.* The Hague: Mouton, 1957.

Chomsky, N. On certain formal properties of grammars. *Information and Control,* 1959, **1**, 91–112.

Chomsky, N. *Aspects of a Theory of Syntax.* Cambridge, Mass.: MIT Press, 1965.

Chomsky, N. Deep structure, surface structure and semantic interpretation. In D. Steinberg and J. Jacobovits (eds.), *Semantics.* Cambridge: Cambridge University Press, 1971.

Clarke, D.D. The structural analysis of verbal interaction. Oxford University: Unpublished doctoral dissertation. 1975.

Cohen, J. Do illocutionary forces exist? *Philosophical Quarterly,* 1964, **14**, 118–37.

Collett, P. and Marsh, P. Patterns of public behaviour: collision avoidance on a pedestrian crossing. *Semiotica,* 1974, **12** (4), 281–99.

Collis, G.M. and Schaffer, H.R. Synchronisation of visual attention in mother-infant pairs. *Journal of Child Psychology and Psychiatry,* 1975, **16** (4), 318–20.

Corcoran, D.W.J. *Pattern recognition.* Harmondsworth: Penguin, 1971.

Cromer, R.F. The development of language and cognition: the cognition hypothesis. In B. Foss (ed.), *New perspectives in child development.* Harmondsworth: Penguin, 1974a.

Cromer, R.F. An experimental investigation of a putative linguistic universal: marking and the indirect object. Mimeo, 1974b.

Dickman, H.R. The perception of behavioural units. In R.G. Barker (ed.), *The stream of behaviour.* New York: Appleton-Century-Crofts, 1963.

Dore, J. *The development of speech acts.* The Hague: Mouton, in press.

Douglas, M. *Natural symbols.* London: The Cresset Press, 1970.

Durkheim, E. *Suicide* (trans. J. Spaulding & G. Simpson). New York: Free Press, 1951 (orig. 1897).

Durkheim, E. *The elementary forms of religious life.* London: George Allen & Unwin, 1971 (orig. 1912).

Durkheim, E. and Mauss, M. *Primitive classification* (trans. R. Needham). London: Cohen & West, 1963 (orig. 1903).

Elkonin, D.B. Development of speech. In A.V. Zaporozhets & D.B. Elkonin (eds.), *The psychology of preschool children.* Cambridge, Mass.: MIT Press, 1971.

Ervin-Tripp, S.M. Sociolinguistics. In L. Berkowitz (ed.), *Advances in experimental social psychology,* vol. 4, 1969.

Espinas, A. *Des sociétés animales.* Paris: These, 1877.

Evans-Pritchard, E.E. *Social anthropology.* London: Cohen & West, 1951.

Evans-Pritchard, E.E. *Nuer religion.* Oxford: Clarendon Press, 1956.

Ferre, F. *Language, logic and God.* London: Collis, 1970.

Fillmore, C.J. The case for case. In E. Bach & R.T. Harmes (eds.), *Universals in linguistic theory.* New York: Holt, Rinehart & Winston, 1968.

Fodor, J.A. and Bever, T. The psychological reality of linguistic segments. *Journal of Verbal Learning and Verbal Behaviour,* 1956, **4**, 414–20.

Fox, R. *Kinship and marriage.* Harmondsworth: Penguin, 1967.

Frake, C.O. How to ask for a drink in Subanun. *American Anthropologist,* 1964, **66**, 127–32.

Frazer, J.G. *The golden bough.* London: Macmillan, 1890.

Fries, C.C. *The structure of English.* New York: Harcourt, Brace & Co., 1952.

Ganz, J.F. *Rules: a systematic analysis.* The Hague: Mouton, 1971.

Gardner, R.A. and Gardner, B.T. *Teaching sign language to a chimpanzee.* University of Nevada Research Report, July 1968.

Gardner, R. and Heider, K.G. *The gardens of war.* Harmondsworth: Penguin, 1974.

Garfinkel, H. A conception of, and experiments with 'trust' as a condition of stable concerted actions. In O.J. Harvey (ed.), *Motivation and social interaction; cognitive determinants.* New York: Ronald Press, 1963.

Garfinkel, H. *Studies in ethnomethodology.* Englewood Cliffs, N.J.: Prentice-Hall, 1967.

Geertz, C. Religion as a cultural system. In M. Banton (ed.), *Anthropological approaches to the study of religion.* (ASA Monograph No. 3) London: Tavistock, 1966.

Gibbs, J.P. Norms: the problem of definition and classification. *American Journal of Sociology,* 1965, **70,** 586–94.

Goffman, E. *Asylums.* Harmondsworth: Penguin, 1970.

Goffman, E. *Relations in public.* London: Allen Lane, 1971.

Goodenough, W. Componential analysis. *Science,* 1967, **156,** 1203–9.

Greenberg, J.H. Some universals of grammar with particular reference to the order of meaningful elements. In J.H. Greenberg (ed.), *Universals of Language.* Cambridge, Mass.: MIT Press, 1963.

Greenfield, P.M. and Smith, J.H. *The structure of communication in early language development.* New York: Academic Press, 1976.

Grice, P. Logic and conversation (The William James Lectures, Harvard University, 1967–8). In P. Cole & J. Morgan (eds.), *Syntax and semantics,* vol. 3, Speech Acts. New York: Academic Press, 1976.

Grice, H.P. Utterer's meaning, sentence-meaning and word-meaning. *Foundations of Language,* 1968, **4,** 225–42.

Gumb, R.D. *Rule-governed linguistic behaviour.* The Hague: Mouton, 1972.

Hallpike, C.R. Is there a primitive mentality? *Times Higher Educational Supplement,* 7 Nov. 1975.

Harré, R. and Secord, P.F. *The explanation of social behaviour.* Oxford: Blackwell, 1972.

Hart, H.L.A. *The concept of law.* Oxford: Clarendon Press, 1961.

Heelas, P.L.F. Intellectualism and the anthropology of religion. Unpublished D.Phil. Thesis, Oxford, 1974a.

Heelas, P.L.F. Meaning and primitive religion. *Journal of the Anthropological Society of Oxford,* 1974b, **5** (2), 80–91.

Hobbes, T. *Leviathan.* New York: Liebal Arts Press, 1958 (orig. 1642).

Hockett, C.F. The problem of universals in language. In J.F. Greenberg (ed.), *Universals of Language,* Cambridge, Mass.: MIT Press, 1963.

Holding, D.H. *Principles of training.* Oxford: Pergamon, 1966.

Humbolt, W. von. *Über die Verschiedenheit des Menschlichen Sprachbaues.* Berlin, 1836.

Hume, D. *A treatise of human nature.* Oxford: Oxford University Press, 1739.

Hunt, E.B., Marin, J. and Store, P.J. *Experiments in induction.* New York: Academic Press, 1966.

Hymes, D. Sociolinguistics and the ethnography of speaking. In E. Ardener (ed.), *Social anthropology and language.* London: Tavistock Publications (ASA Monograph 10), 1971.

Jakobson, R. Implication of language universals for linguistics. In J.H. Greenberg (ed.), *Universals of Language.* Cambridge, Mass.: MIT Press, 1963.

Jakobson, R. *Child language, aphasia and general sound laws.* The Hague: Mouton, 1968.

Jakobson, R. *Collected papers.* The Hague, Mouton, 1972.

Jarvie, I.C. *Concepts and society.* London: Routledge & Kegan Paul, 1972.

Jarvie, I.C. and Agassi, J. The problem of rationality of magic. In B. Wilson (ed.), *Rationality.* Oxford: Blackwell, 1970.

Johnson, N.F. The psychological reality of phrase structure rules. *Journal of Verbal Learning and Verbal Behaviour,* 1965, **4**, 469–75.

Kant, I. *Critique of pure reason.* London: Macmillan, 1961 (orig. 1781).

Kintsch, W. *Learning, memory and conceptual processes.* New York: Wiley, 1970.

Kohlberg, L. and Kramer, R. Continuities and discontinuities in childhood and adult moral development. *Human Development,* 1969, **12**, 93–120.

Laguna, G. de. *Speech; its function and development.* Bloomington, Ind.: Indiana University Press, 1963 (orig. 1927).

Lakoff, G. On generative semantics. In D. Steinberg and J. Jakobovits (eds.), *Semantics.* Cambridge: Cambridge University Press, 1971.

Leach, E.R. *Political systems of Highland Burma.* London: Athlone Press, 1954.

Leach, E.R. *Pul Elyia; a village in Ceylon.* Cambridge: Cambridge University Press, 1961.

Leach, E.R. *Genesis as myth.* London: Jonathan Cape, 1969.

Leech, C. *Semantics.* Harmondsworth: Penguin, 1975.

Lévi-Strauss, C. The bear and the barber. *Journal of the Royal Anthropological Institute,* 1963, **93**, 1–11.

Lévi-Strauss, C. *The savage mind.* London: Weidenfeld & Nicolson, 1966.

Lévi-Strauss, C. *Structural anthropology* (trans. C. Jacobson & B.G. Schoeff). Harmondsworth: Penguin, 1968.

Lévi-Strauss, C. *Totemism.* Harmondsworth: Penguin, 1969.

Lévi-Strauss, C. *The elementary structures of kinship* (trans. J.H. Bell, J.R. von Sturmer & R. Needham, ed.). Boston: Beacon Press, 1969 (orig. 1949).

Lewis, D. *Convention; a philosophical study.* Cambridge, Mass.: Harvard University Press, 1969.

Lewis, I.M. *Ecstatic religion.* Harmondsworth: Penguin, 1971.

Liberman, A.M., Harris, K.C., Hoffman, M.S. & Griffith, B.C. The discrimination of speech sounds within and across phoneme boundaries. *Journal of Experimental Psychology,* 1957, **54**, 358–68.

Lienhardt, G. *Divinity and Experience.* Oxford: Clarendon Press, 1961.

Light, L.L. and Carter-Sobell, L. Effects of changed semantic context on recognition memory. *Journal of Verbal Learning and Verbal Behaviour,* 1970, **9**, 1–11.

Lyman, S. and Scott, M. *A sociology of the absurd.* New York: Appleton-Century-Crofts, 1970.

MacClay, H. Overview. In D. Steinberg and J. Jacobovits (eds.), *Semantics.* Cambridge: Cambridge University Press, 1971.

MacIntyre, A. A mistake about causality in the social sciences. In P. Laslett & W. Runciman (eds.), *Philosophy, politics and society.* Oxford: Blackwell, 1962.

MacIntyre, A. The idea of a social science. *The Aristotelian Society,* Supplementary volume XLI, 1967.

MacIntyre, A. Is understanding religion compatible with believing? In B. Wilson (ed.), *Rationality.* Oxford: Blackwell, 1970a.

MacIntyre, A. The logical status of religious beliefs. In S. Toulmin, R. Hepburn & A. MacIntyre (eds.), *Metaphysical beliefs.* London: SCM Press, 1970b.

MacIntyre, A. *Against the self-images of the age.* London: Duckworth, 1971.

Mackworth, N.H. and Bruner, J.S. How adults and children search and recognize pictures. *Human Development,* 1970, **13**, 149–77.

Malcolm, N. *Problems of mind.* London: George Allen & Unwin, 1972.

Malinowski, B. *The sexual life of savages.* London: Routledge, 1922.

Maratos, O. Development of imitation. Paper presented at the British Psychological Society Conference, 1973.

McBride, G., Parer, I.P. and Foenander, F. The social organization and behaviour of the feral domestic fowl. *Animal Behaviour Monographs,* 1969, **2** (3), 125–81.

McCawley, J.D. The role of semantics in a grammar. In E. Bach and R.T. Harmes (eds.), *Universals in linguistic theory.* New York: Holt, Rinehart & Winston, 1968.

McNeill, D. *The acquisition of language.* New York: Harper & Row, 1970.

McNeill, D. Semiotic extension. Paper presented at the Loyola Symposium on Cognition, 30 April 1974, Chicago.

Mead, G.H. *Mind, self and society* (ed. C.W. Morris). Chicago: University of Chicago Press, 1934.

Mill, J.S. *A system of logic, ratiocinative and inductive.* London: Parker, 1851.

Miller, G.A., Galanter, E. and Pribram, K.L. *Plans and the structure of behaviour.* New York: Holt, Rinehart & Winston, 1960.

Mischel, T. (ed.) *Understanding other persons.* Oxford: Blackwell, 1975.

Moscovici, S. Society and theory in social psychology. In J. Israel and H. Tajfel (eds.), *The context of social psychology.* London: Academic Press, 1972.

Nadel, S.F. *Nupe religion.* London: Routledge & Kegan Paul, 1954.

Needham, R. *Structure and sentiment.* London: University of Chicago Press, 1962.

Neisser, N. *Cognitive psychology.* New York: Appleton-Century-Crofts, 1967.

Nelson, K. Structure and strategy in learning to talk. *Society for Research in Child Development Monographs,* 1973, **38** (1–2: Serial no. 149).

Newtson, D. Attribution and the perception of ongoing behaviour. *Journal of Personality and Social Psychology,* 1973, **28**, 28–38.

O'Brien, C.C. *Parnell and his party.* Oxford: Clarendon Press, 1957.

Odum, E.P. *Fundamentals of ecology.* Philadelphia: Saunders, 1971.

Osgood, C.E. Interpersonal verbs and interpersonal behaviour. Report from Group Effectiveness Research Laboratory, University of Illinois, 1968.

Osgood, C.E. Speculation on the structure of interpersonal intuition. *Behavioural Science*, 1970, **15**, 237–54.

Otto, R. *The idea of the holy.* London: Oxford University Press, 1958.

Parsons, T. *The structure of social action.* London: Collier-Macmillan, 1968.

Pease, K. and Arnold, P. Approximations to dialogue. *American Journal of Psychology*, 1973, **86**, 769–76.

Piaget, J. *The moral judgement of the child.* London: Routledge & Kegan Paul, 1932.

Pike, K.L. *Language in relation to a unified theory of the structure of human behaviour.* The Hague: Mouton, 1967.

Popper, K. *Conjectures and refutations.* London: Routledge, 1968.

Quine, W.V.O. *Word and object.* Cambridge, Mass.: MIT Press, 1960.

Quine, W.V.O. Some methodological reflections on current linguistic theory. In G. Harman and D. Davidson (eds.), *The semantics of natural language.* Dordrecht-Holland: D. Reidel, 1972.

Radcliffe-Brown, A.R. *Structure and function in primitive society.* London; Cohen & West, 1952.

Ramsey, I.T. *Religious language.* London: SCM Press, 1957.

Raush, H.L. Process and change—a markov model for interaction. *Family Process*, 1972, **11**, 275–98.

Reynolds, P.C. Play, language and human evolution. In J. Bruner, A. Jolly & K. Sylva (eds.), *Play; its role in evolution and development.* Harmondsworth: Penguin, 1976.

Rheingold, H.L., Gewirtz, J. and Ross, H. Social conditioning of vocalization in the infant. *Journal of Comparative Physiological Psychology*, 1959, **52**, 68–73.

Richards, I.A. *Mencius on the mind.* London: Routledge & Kegan Paul, 1964.

Robinson, W.P. *Language and social behaviour.* Harmondsworth: Penguin, 1972.

Robson, K.S. The role of eye-to-eye contact in maternal–infant attachment. Child Research Branch, NIMH, Bethesda, Maryland, 1967.

Rommetveit, R. *Social norms and roles.* Minneapolis: University of Minnesota Press, 1955.

Rosenthal, R. *Experimentor effects in behavioural research.* New York: Appleton-Century-Crofts, 1968.

Ross, J.R. On declarative utterances. In R. Jacobs and P. Rosenbaum (eds.), *Readings in English transformational grammar.* Waltham: Gunn & Co., 1970.

Ryan, A. *The philosophy of the social sciences.* London: Macmillan, 1970.

Ryan, J. Early language development. In M.P.M. Richards (ed.), *The integration of the child into a social world.* Cambridge: Cambridge University Press, 1974.

Saussure, F. de. *Cours de linguistique générale.* Paris: Payot, 1916.

Schegloff, E.A. Sequencing in conversational openings. *American Anthropologist,* 1968, **70,** 1075–95.

Schlesinger, I.M. Relational concepts underlying language. In R.L. Schiefelbusch & L.I. Lloyd (eds.), *Language perspectives; acquisition, retardation and intervention.* London: Macmillan, 1974.

Schutz, A.J. *Collected papers* (ed. Maurice-Natanson & I. Schutz). The Hague: Martinus–Nijhoff, 1962–6.

Schwayder, D.S. *The stratification of behaviour.* London: Routledge, 1965.

Searle, J. What is a speech act? In M. Black (ed.), *Philosophy in America.* New York: Allen & Unwin and Cornell University Press, 1965.

Searle, J. Austin on locutionary and illocutionary acts. *Philosophical Review,* 1968, **77,** 405–24.

Searle, J. *Speech acts.* Cambridge: Cambridge University Press, 1970.

Secord, P. and Blackman, C. *Social psychology.* New York: McGraw-Hill, 1974.

Simmel, G. *The sociology of Georg Simmel* (trans. K. Wolff). Glencoe, Ill.: Free Press, 1950.

Sinclair-de-Zwart, H. Developmental psycholinguistics. In D. Elkind & J.H. Flavell (eds.), *Studies in cognitive development:* Essays in honor of Jean Piaget. New York: Oxford University Press, 1969.

Slater, P.J.B. Describing sequences of behaviour. In P.P.G. Bateson & P.H. Klopfer (eds.), *Perspectives in ethology*. New York: Plenum, 1973.

Slobin, D.I. The acquisition of Russian as a native language. In F. Smith & G.A. Miller (eds.), *The Genesis of language*. Cambridge, Mass.: MIT Press, 1966.

Smart, N. *The science of religion and the sociology of knowledge.* Princeton: Princeton University Press, 1973.

Spencer, H. *Principles of sociology; ceremonial institutions.* London: Williams & Northgate, 1879.

Strawson, P.F. Persons. Chapter 3 in *Individuals*. London: Methuen, 1959.

Sugarman, S. A description of communicative development in the pre-language child. Honors thesis, Hampshire College, 1973.

Tambiah, S.J. Form and meaning of magical acts: a point of view. In R. Horton & R. Finnegan (ed.), *Modes of thought*. London: Faber & Faber, 1973.

Trabasso, T. and Bower, G.H. *Attention in learning; theory and research.* New York: Wiley, 1968.

Trevarthen, C. Infant response to objects and persons. Paper presented at the Spring meeting of the British Psychological Society, Bangor, 1974.

Tyler, S. (ed.) *Cognitive anthropology.* New York: Holt, Rinehart & Winston, 1969.

Ullman, S. Semantic universals. In J.H. Greenberg (ed.), *Universals of Language*. Cambridge, Mass.: MIT Press, 1963.

Urmson, J.O. *Philosophical analysis.* Oxford: Oxford University Press, 1965.

Vanderbilt, A. *The new complete book of etiquette.* New York: Doubleday, 1963.

van Hooff, J.A.R.A.M. A structural analysis of the social behaviour of a semi-captive group of chimpanzees. In M. von Cranach & I. Vine (eds.), *Social Communication and movement*. London: Academic Press, 1973.

Vendler, Z. *Linguistics in philosophy.* New York: Cornell University Press, 1967.

von Wright, G.H. *Norm and action.* London: Routledge, 1963.

Vygotsky, L.S. *Thought and language* (trans. E. Haufmann & G. Vakar). Cambridge, Mass.: MIT Press, 1962 (orig. 1936).

Waismann, F. *Principles of linguistic philosophy* (ed. R. Harré). London: Macmillan, 1965.
Waismann, F. *How I see philosophy* (ed. R. Harré). London: Macmillan, 1968.
Winch, P. Understanding a primitive society. In D.Z. Phillips (ed.), *Religion and understanding.* Oxford: Blackwell, 1967.
Winch, P. *The idea of a social science and its relation to philosophy.* London: Routledge & Kegan Paul, 1971.
Winch, P. *Ethics and action.* London: Routledge & Kegan Paul, 1972.
Wittgenstein, L. *Philosophical investigations* (trans. G.E.M. Anscombe). Oxford: Blackwell, 1953.
Wittgenstein, L. Remarks on Frazer's 'Golden Bough'. *The Human World,* 1971, **3**, 28–41.

Yngve, V.H. I forgot what I was going to say. Papers presented to the ninth regional meeting of the Chicago Linguistic Circle, 1973.

Zajonc, R. Social facilitation. *Science,* 1965, 149, 269–74.
Zajonc, R. Attitudinal effects of mere exposure. *Journal of Personality and Social Psychology, Monograph Supplement,* 1968, **9**, No. 2.
Ziff, P. *Semantic analysis.* Ithaca: Cornell University Press, 1960.

DATE DUE